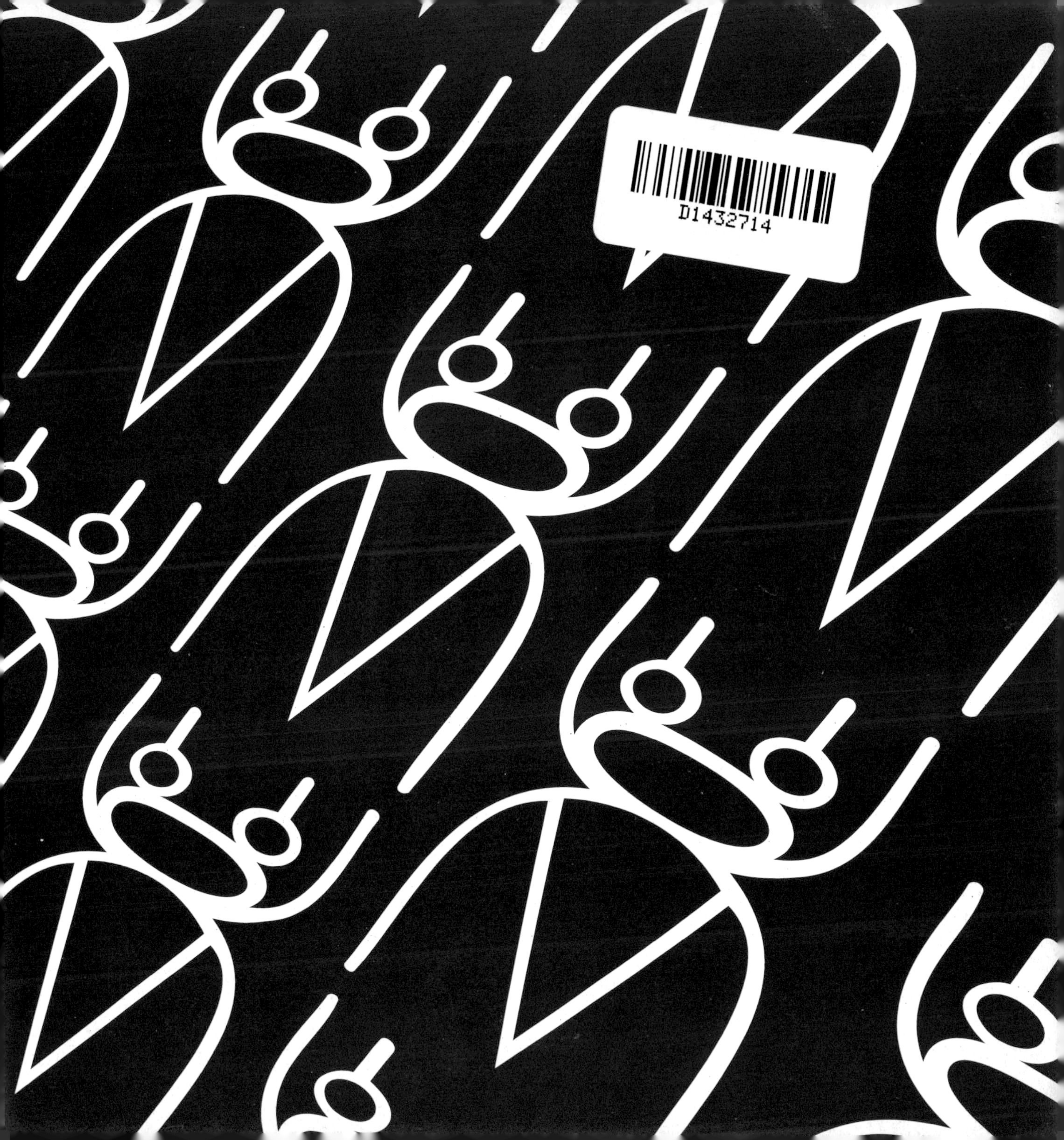

Sponsored by:

A1 Comics .com

ABSTRACT SPROCKET

ArtSTORE

Nice'n'Sleazy
cafe - bar - venue

CITY CENTRE COMICS
GLASGOW'S PREMIER BACK-ISSUE SPECIALIST

GROSVENOR CAFE

THE 13TH NOTE

DEADHEAD COMICS

GRASSROOTS
WHOLEFOOD SUPERMARKET
& ORGANIC OFF LICENCE

CAFÉ GANDOLFI

KING TUTS WAH WAH HUT

QUIGG'S -OF- GLASGOW
PHOTOGRAPHIC & OPTICAL

A1 Books & Comics, 31-35 Parnie Street, Glasgow G1 5RJ. Tel: 0141 552 6692.
635 Great Western Road, Glasgow G12 8RE. Tel: 0141 357 6944.
28 Argyle Street, Glasgow. Tel: 0141 226 5414.
Abstract Sprocket, 29 St Benedict's Street, Norwich NR2 4PF. Tel: 01603 624410.
Art Store, 94 Queen Street, Glasgow G1 3AQ. Tel: 0141 221 1101.
City Centre Comics, 168 Buchanan Street, Glasgow G1 2LW. Tel: 0141 331 1215.
Deadhead Comics, 27 Candlemaker Row, Edinburgh EH1 2QG. Tel: 0131 226 2774.
Café Gandolfi, 64 Albion Street, Glasgow G1 & at Habitat in the Buchanan Galleries, Glasgow. Tel: 0141 552 6813.
Grassroots, 20 Woodlands Road, Charing X, Glasgow G3 6UR. Tel: 0141 353 3278.
The Grosvenor Café, 31 Ashton Lane, Glasgow G12. Tel: 0141 339 1848.
King Tuts Wah Wah Hut, 272 St Vincent Street, Glasgow G2 5RL. Tel: 0141 221 5279.
Nice'n'Sleazy, 421 Sauchiehall Street, Glasgow. Tel: 0141 333 0900.
Quiggs of Glasgow, 7-11 Parnie Street, Glasgow G1 5RJ. Tel: 0141 552 6823.
The 13th Note Café, 50/60 King Street, Glasgow G1 5QT. Tel: 0141 553 1638.
The 13th Note Club, 260 Clyde Street, Glasgow G1 4JH. Tel: 0141 221 0414.

LOUIS
Lying to Clive

by Metaphrog

Also by Metaphrog:

Louis - Red Letter Day
Strange Weather Lately
Vermin
The Maze

Coming soon, more
Louis' adventures!

Louis - *Lying to Clive*
Published by Metaphrog, 34 Springhill Gardens, Shawlands, Glasgow G41 2EY, Scotland.
www.metaphrog.com

Printed in Scotland by Clydeside Press Ltd, 37 High Street, Glasgow G1.

ISBN 09534932 7 X (Paperback)
ISBN 09534932 6 1 (Hardback)

LOUIS

Lying to Clive

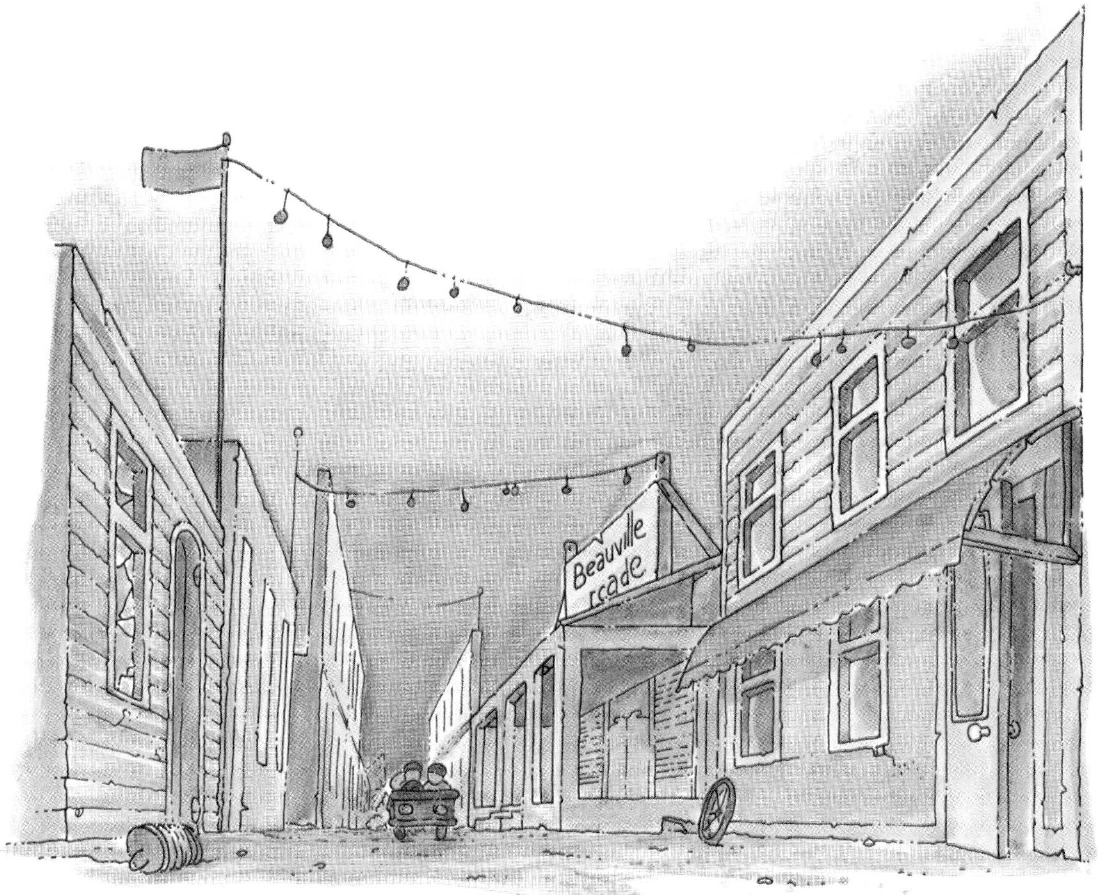
Beauville
rcade

by **Metaphrog**

LEAVING HAMLET, LOUIS HAD WATCHED THE SCENERY CHANGE. AND NOW, TRAVELLING THROUGH THE DUSTY, DESERTED STREETS HE REALISED THAT BEAUVILLE WAS NOT PARTICULARLY BEAUTIFUL. IN FACT, IT WASN'T REALLY A TOWN AT ALL. NOTHING WAS QUITE AS IT SEEMED.

PERHAPS THIS PLACE HAD ONCE SERVED A PURPOSE? LOUIS WONDERED IF IT WAS SOMEONE ELSE'S IDEA OF BEAUTY...

... BUT HIS HEART FELT HEAVY AND HE DIDN'T FEEL INCLINED TO ASK.

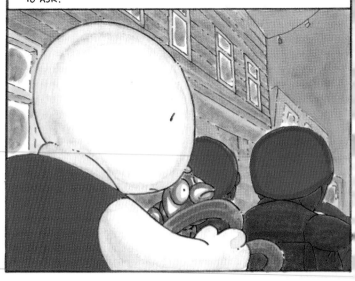

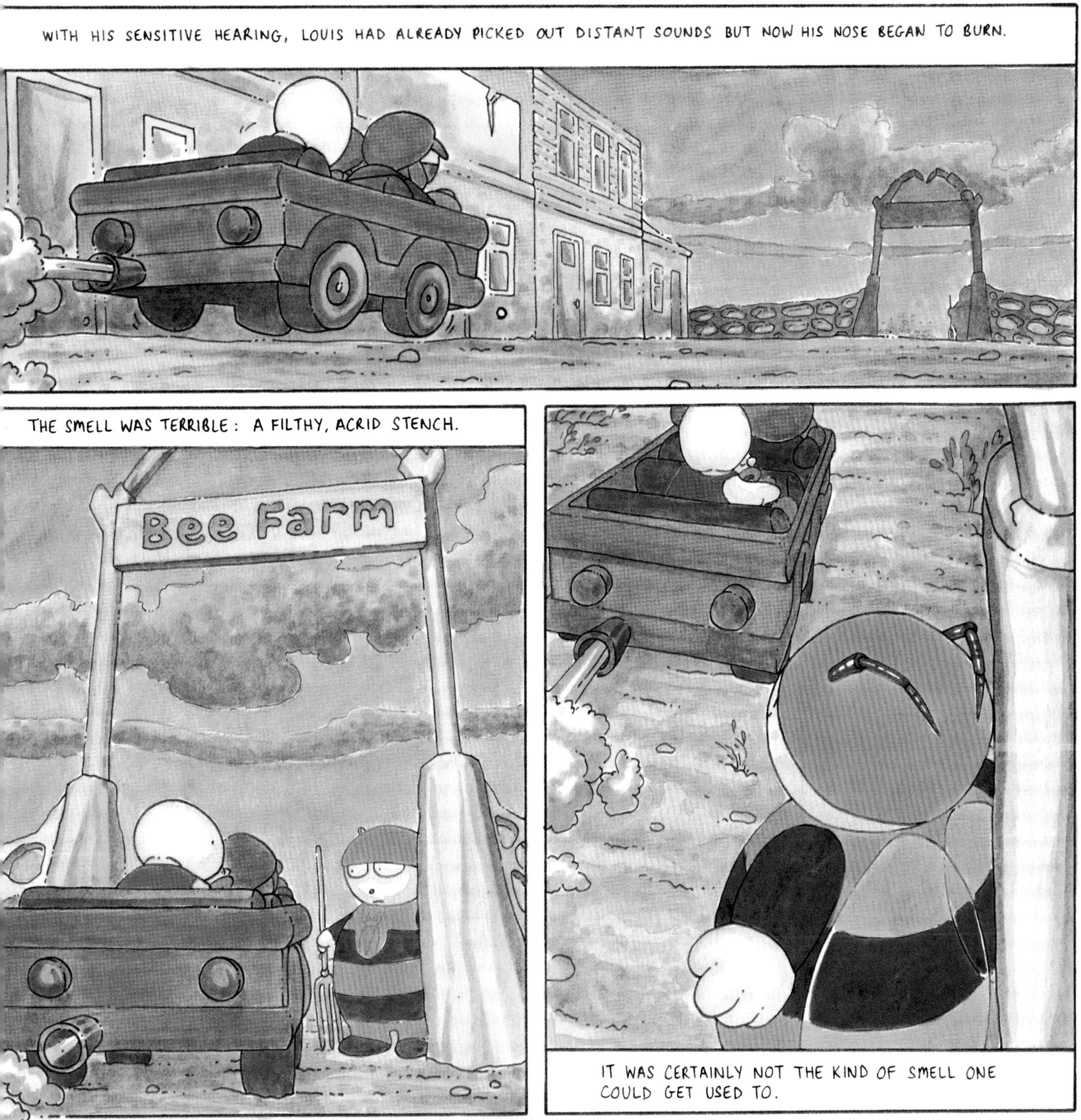
WITH HIS SENSITIVE HEARING, LOUIS HAD ALREADY PICKED OUT DISTANT SOUNDS BUT NOW HIS NOSE BEGAN TO BURN.
THE SMELL WAS TERRIBLE: A FILTHY, ACRID STENCH.
Bee Farm
IT WAS CERTAINLY NOT THE KIND OF SMELL ONE COULD GET USED TO.

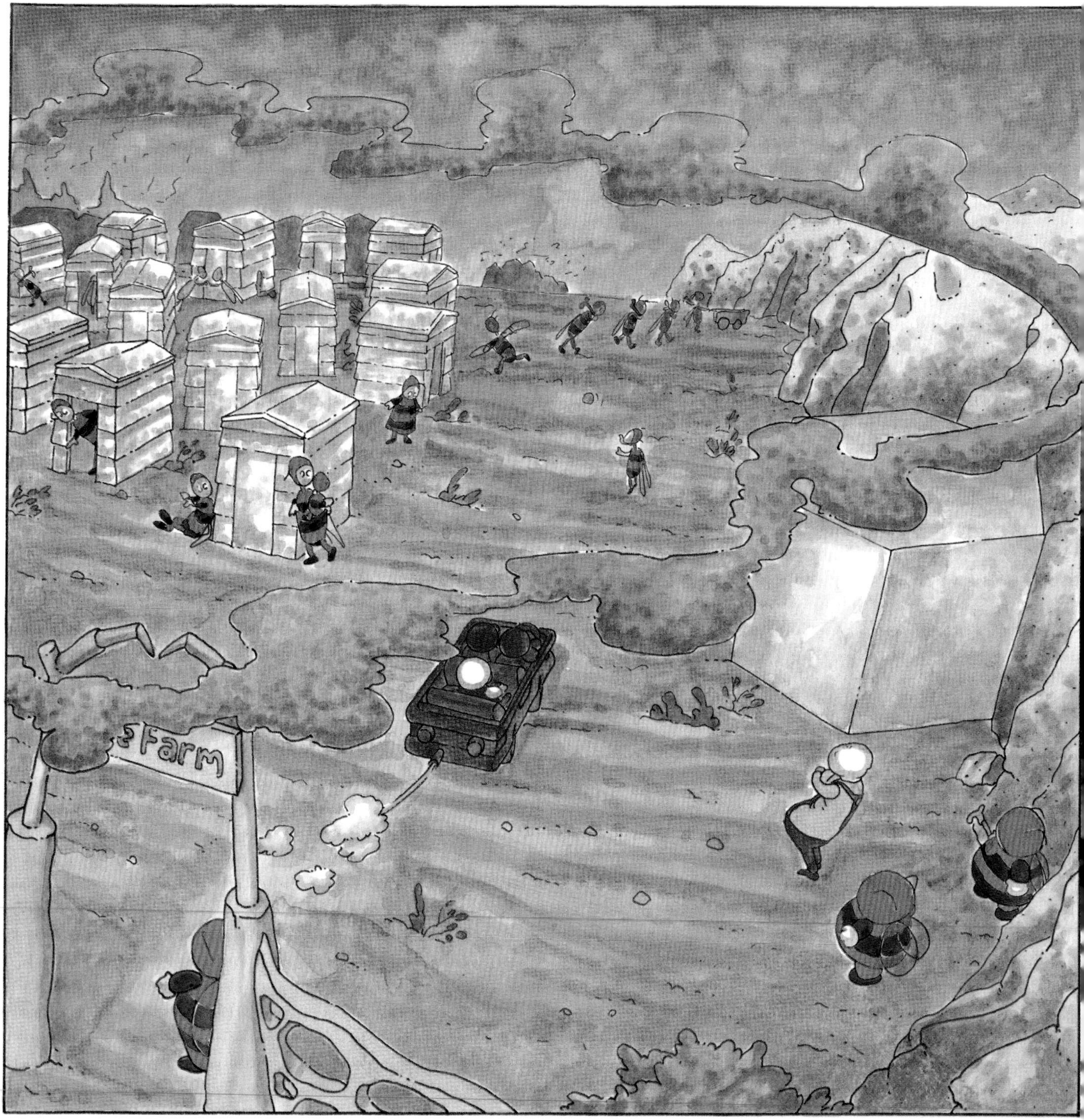
Farm

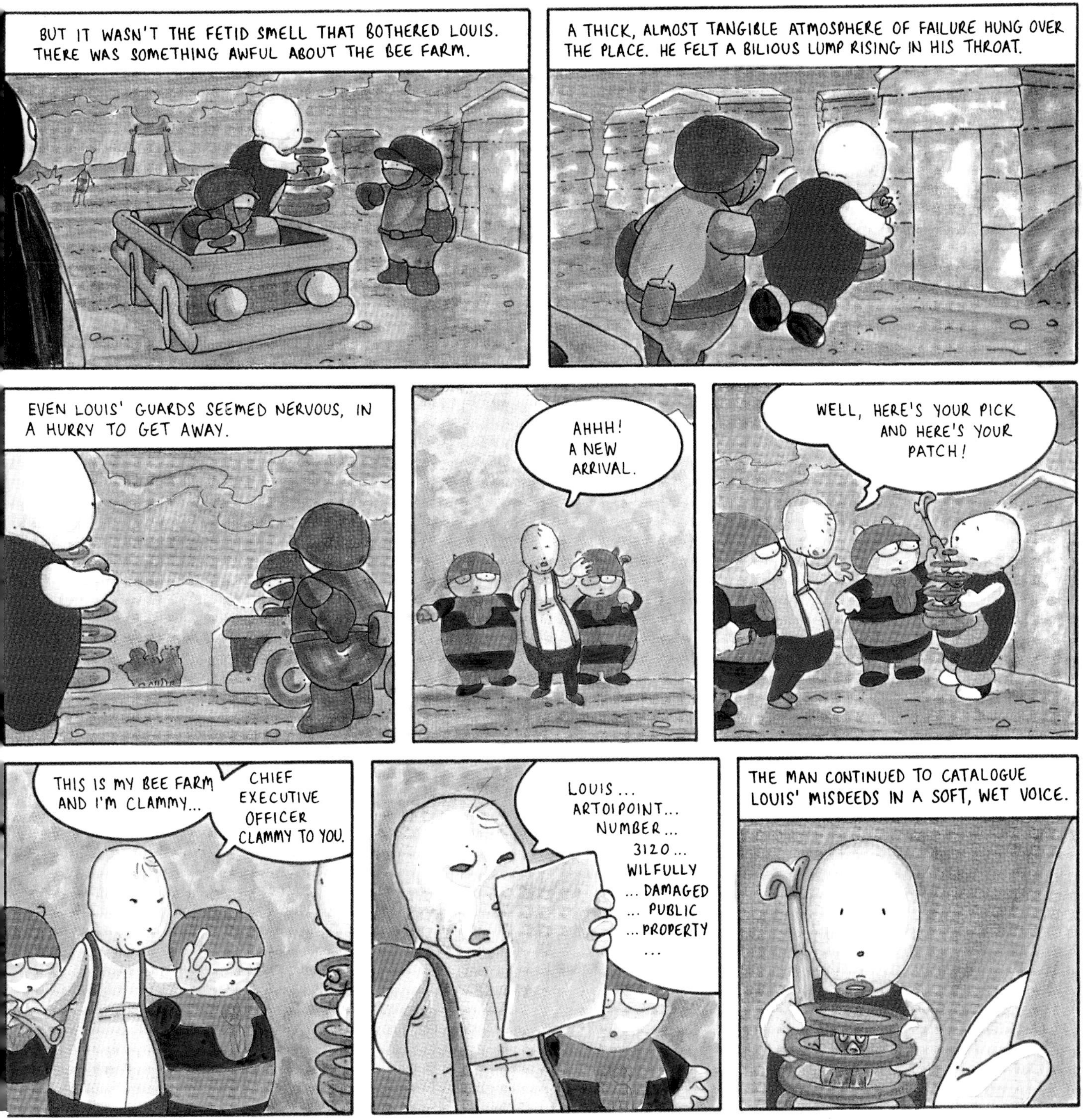
BUT IT WASN'T THE FETID SMELL THAT BOTHERED LOUIS. THERE WAS SOMETHING AWFUL ABOUT THE BEE FARM.
A THICK, ALMOST TANGIBLE ATMOSPHERE OF FAILURE HUNG OVER THE PLACE. HE FELT A BILIOUS LUMP RISING IN HIS THROAT.
EVEN LOUIS' GUARDS SEEMED NERVOUS, IN A HURRY TO GET AWAY.
AHHH! A NEW ARRIVAL.
WELL, HERE'S YOUR PICK AND HERE'S YOUR PATCH!
THIS IS MY BEE FARM AND I'M CLAMMY...
CHIEF EXECUTIVE OFFICER CLAMMY TO YOU.
LOUIS... ARTOIPOINT... NUMBER... 3120... WILFULLY ... DAMAGED ... PUBLIC ... PROPERTY ...
THE MAN CONTINUED TO CATALOGUE LOUIS' MISDEEDS IN A SOFT, WET VOICE.

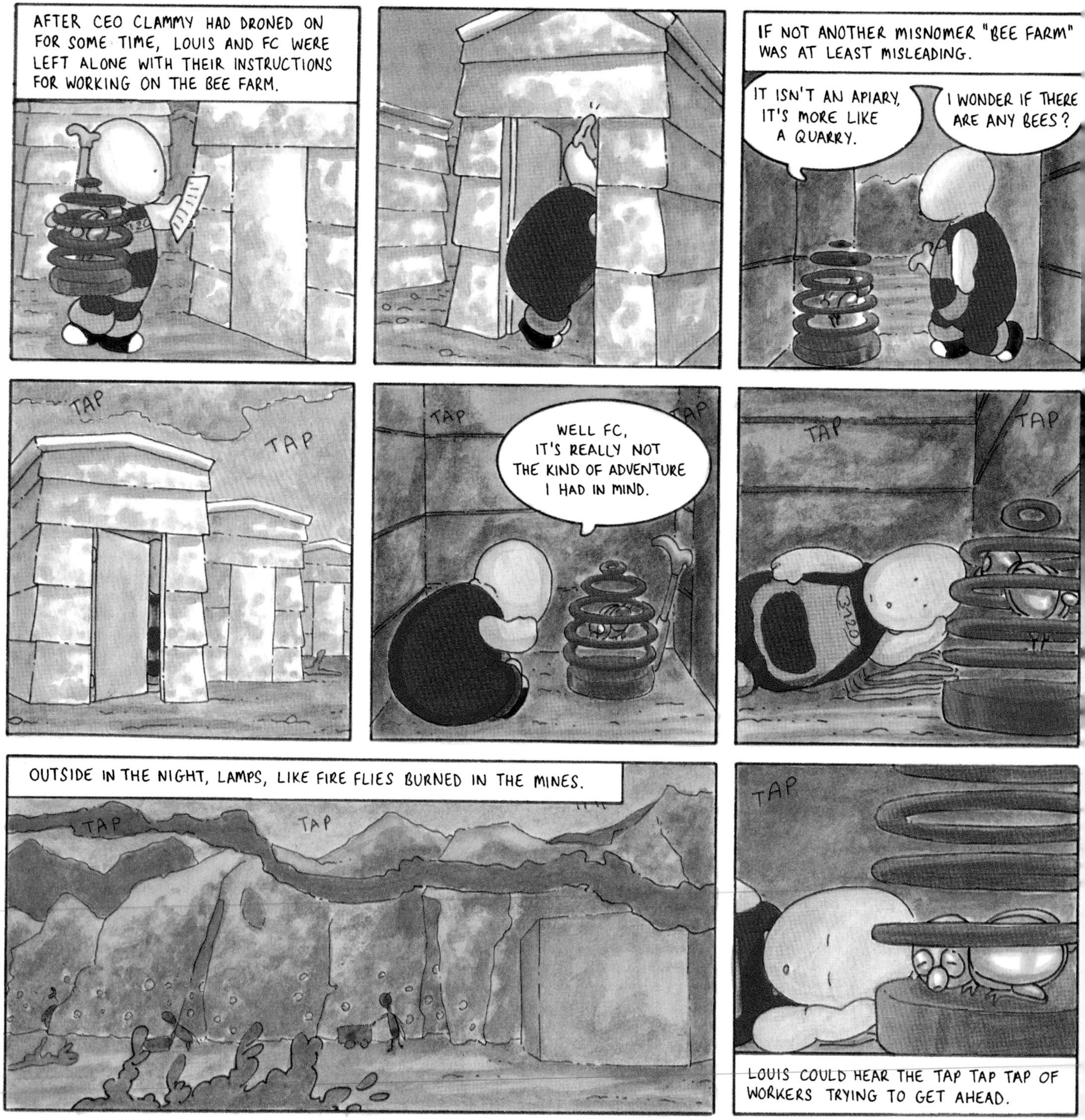
AFTER CEO CLAMMY HAD DRONED ON FOR SOME TIME, LOUIS AND FC WERE LEFT ALONE WITH THEIR INSTRUCTIONS FOR WORKING ON THE BEE FARM.
IF NOT ANOTHER MISNOMER "BEE FARM" WAS AT LEAST MISLEADING.
IT ISN'T AN APIARY, IT'S MORE LIKE A QUARRY.
I WONDER IF THERE ARE ANY BEES?
TAP
TAP
TAP
WELL FC, IT'S REALLY NOT THE KIND OF ADVENTURE I HAD IN MIND.
TAP
TAP
OUTSIDE IN THE NIGHT, LAMPS, LIKE FIRE FLIES BURNED IN THE MINES.
TAP
TAP
TAP
LOUIS COULD HEAR THE TAP TAP TAP OF WORKERS TRYING TO GET AHEAD.

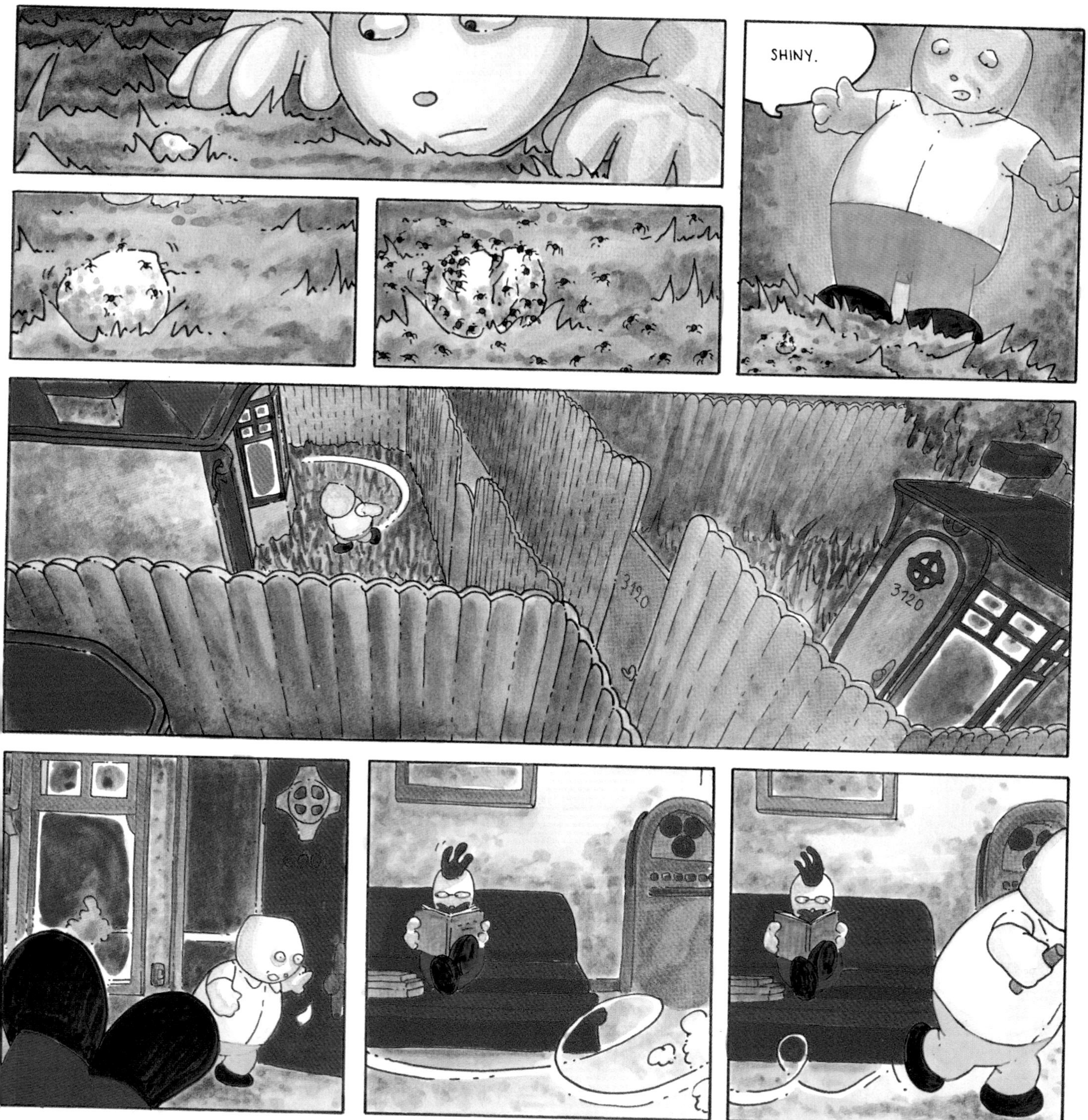

SHINY.
3120
3120

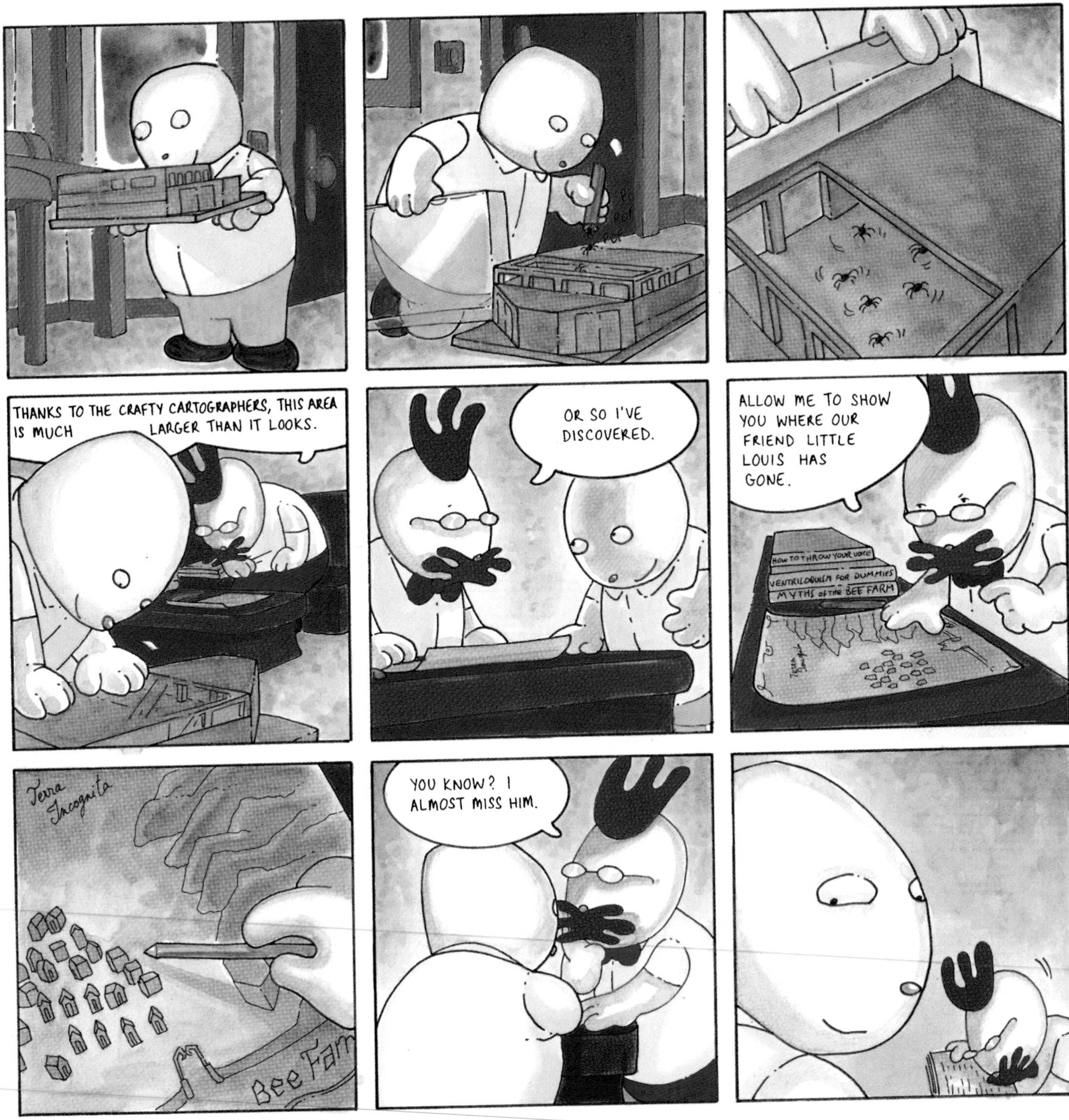
THANKS TO THE CRAFTY CARTOGRAPHERS, THIS AREA IS MUCH LARGER THAN IT LOOKS.
OR SO I'VE DISCOVERED.
ALLOW ME TO SHOW YOU WHERE OUR FRIEND LITTLE LOUIS HAS GONE.
HOW TO THROW YOUR VOICE
VENTRILOQUISM FOR DUMMIES
MYTHS of the BEE FARM
Terra Incognita
Bee Farm
YOU KNOW? I ALMOST MISS HIM.

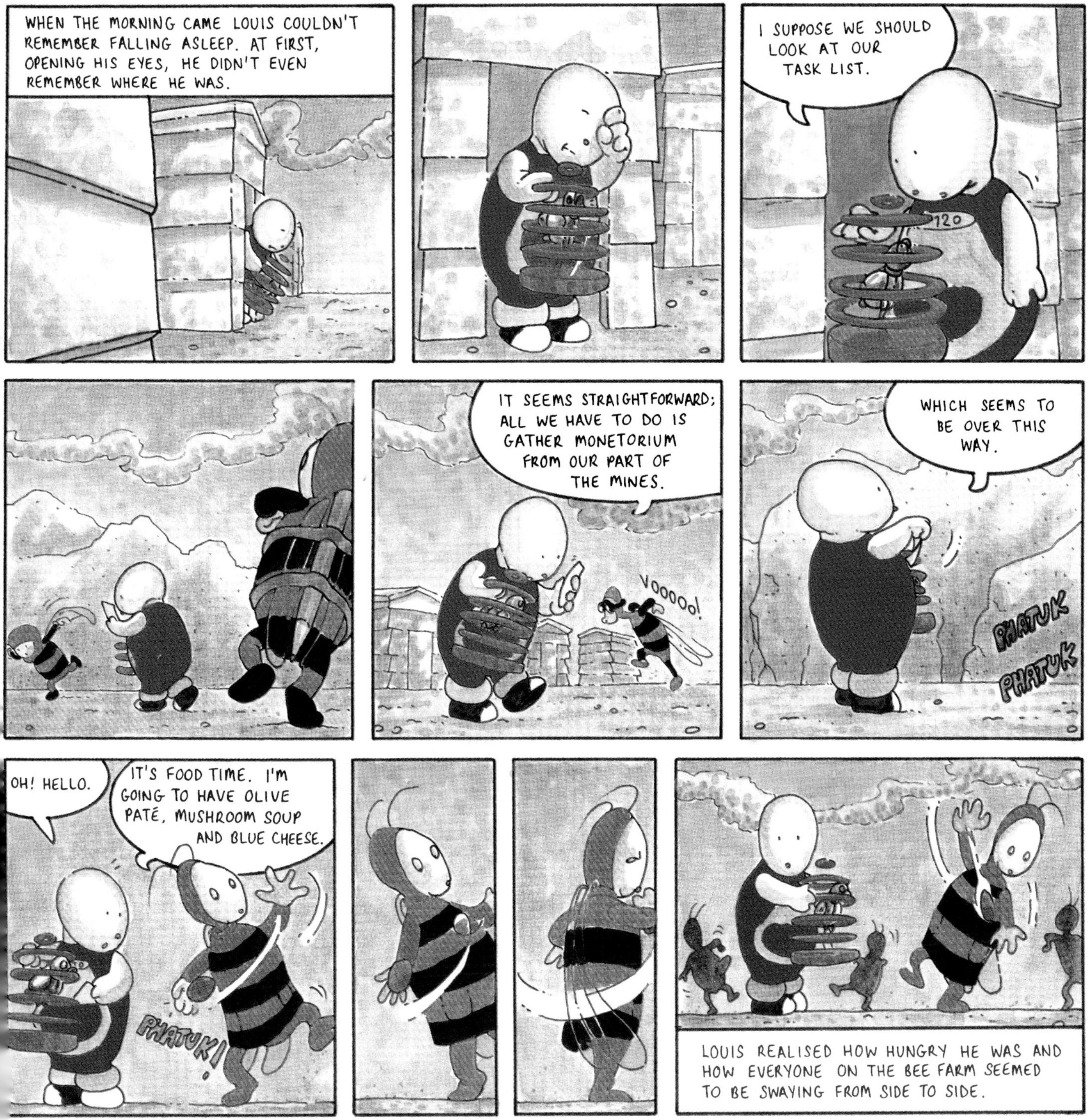
WHEN THE MORNING CAME LOUIS COULDN'T REMEMBER FALLING ASLEEP. AT FIRST, OPENING HIS EYES, HE DIDN'T EVEN REMEMBER WHERE HE WAS.
I SUPPOSE WE SHOULD LOOK AT OUR TASK LIST.
120
IT SEEMS STRAIGHTFORWARD; ALL WE HAVE TO DO IS GATHER MONETORIUM FROM OUR PART OF THE MINES.
VOOOOO!
WHICH SEEMS TO BE OVER THIS WAY.
PHATUK
PHATUK
OH! HELLO.
IT'S FOOD TIME. I'M GOING TO HAVE OLIVE PATÉ, MUSHROOM SOUP AND BLUE CHEESE.
PHATUK!
LOUIS REALISED HOW HUNGRY HE WAS AND HOW EVERYONE ON THE BEE FARM SEEMED TO BE SWAYING FROM SIDE TO SIDE.

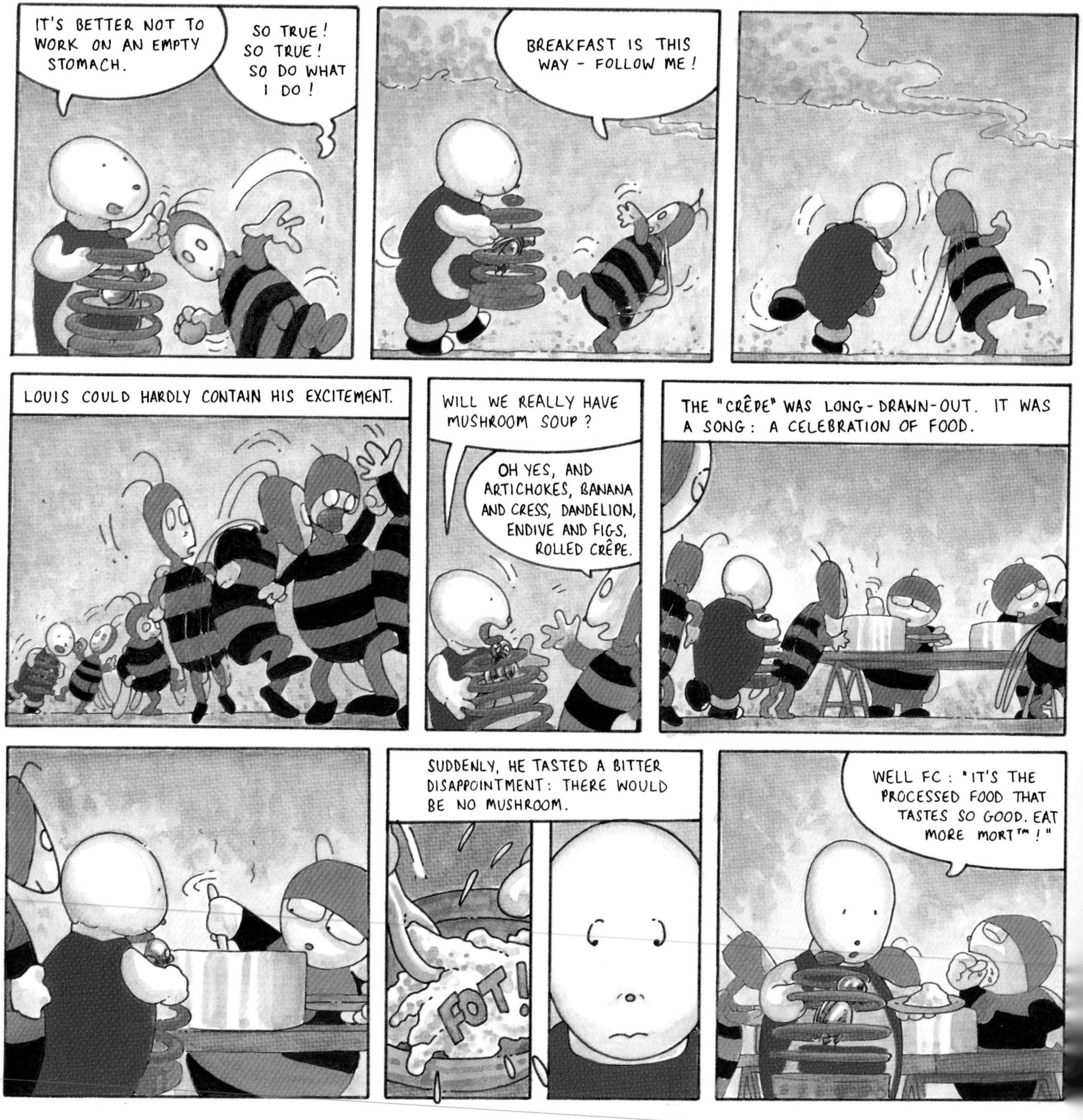
IT'S BETTER NOT TO WORK ON AN EMPTY STOMACH.
SO TRUE! SO TRUE! SO DO WHAT I DO!
BREAKFAST IS THIS WAY - FOLLOW ME!
LOUIS COULD HARDLY CONTAIN HIS EXCITEMENT.
WILL WE REALLY HAVE MUSHROOM SOUP?
OH YES, AND ARTICHOKES, BANANA AND CRESS, DANDELION, ENDIVE AND FIGS, ROLLED CRÊPE.
THE "CRÊPE" WAS LONG-DRAWN-OUT. IT WAS A SONG: A CELEBRATION OF FOOD.
SUDDENLY, HE TASTED A BITTER DISAPPOINTMENT: THERE WOULD BE NO MUSHROOM.
FOT!
WELL FC: "IT'S THE PROCESSED FOOD THAT TASTES SO GOOD. EAT MORE MORT™!"

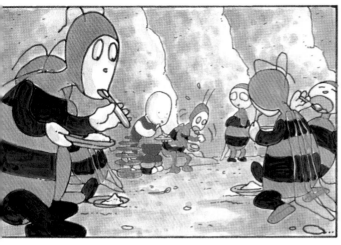

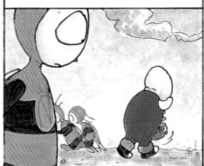

LOUIS WASN'T SURE IF IT WAS DISAPPOINTMENT OR INDIGESTION THAT MADE HIM FEEL QUEASY AS HE RETURNED TOWARDS THE MINES.
TAC TAC TAC TAC TAC TAC
TAC
AFTER CHIPPING AWAY AT THE VARIEGATED FACE FOR SOME TIME LOUIS' NAUSEA HAD DISAPPEARED.
IT'S EXQUISITELY VEINED, LIKE A LEAF. QUITE BEAUTIFUL.
3120
ALTHOUGH, I'VE NEVER SEEN LEAVES LIKE THAT IN OUR GARDEN.
3120
LOUIS REALISED THAT HE MISSED HAMLET MORE THAN A LITTLE.
ACCORDING TO THE INSTRUCTIONS WE SHOULD MOVE THIS PILE TO THE GARBAGE AREA.
3120

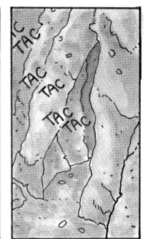

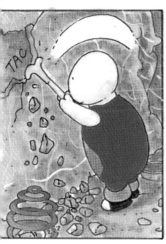

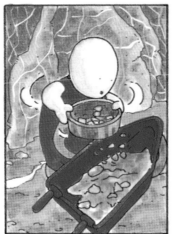

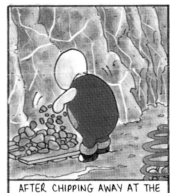

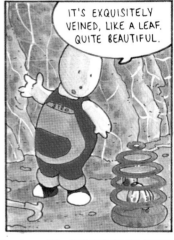

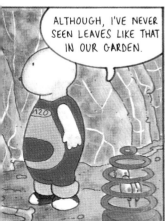

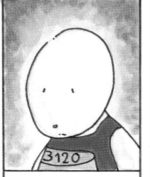

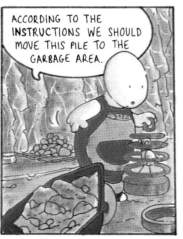

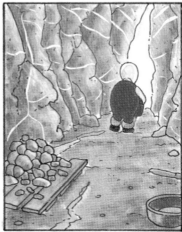

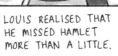

MUSN'T MISS OUT ON YOUR SUCK STRIPES!

SUCK STRIPES?

COME ON FC, WE'D BETTER GET BACK TO WORK!

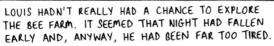

LOUIS HADN'T REALLY HAD A CHANCE TO EXPLORE THE BEE FARM. IT SEEMED THAT NIGHT HAD FALLEN EARLY AND, ANYWAY, HE HAD BEEN FAR TOO TIRED.

WELL, THAT CERTAINLY EXPLAINS THE SMELL.

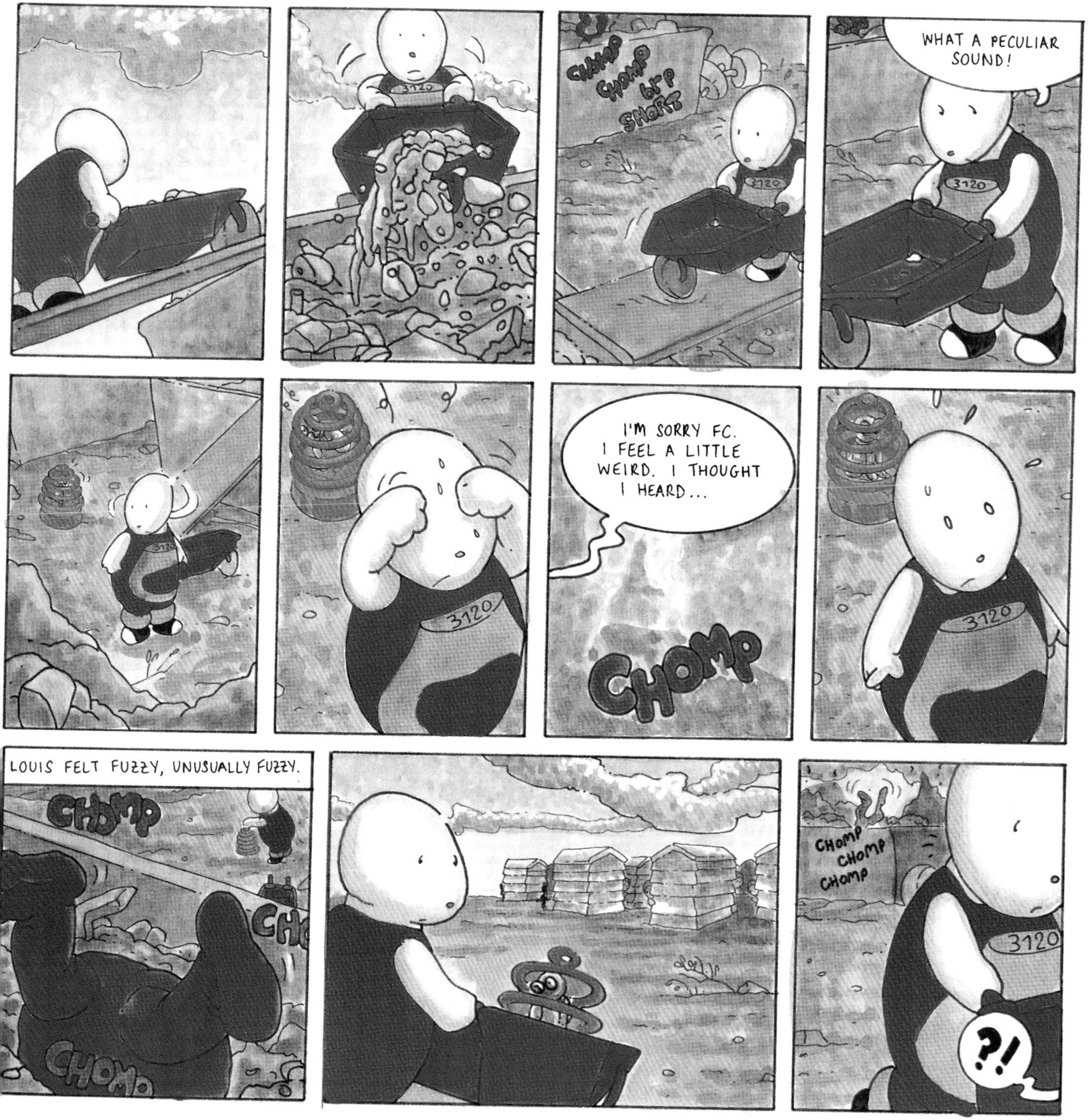
CHOMP CHOMP brp SHORT
WHAT A PECULIAR SOUND!
I'M SORRY FC. I FEEL A LITTLE WEIRD. I THOUGHT I HEARD...
CHOMP
LOUIS FELT FUZZY, UNUSUALLY FUZZY.
CHOMP
CHOMP CHOMP CHOMP
?!

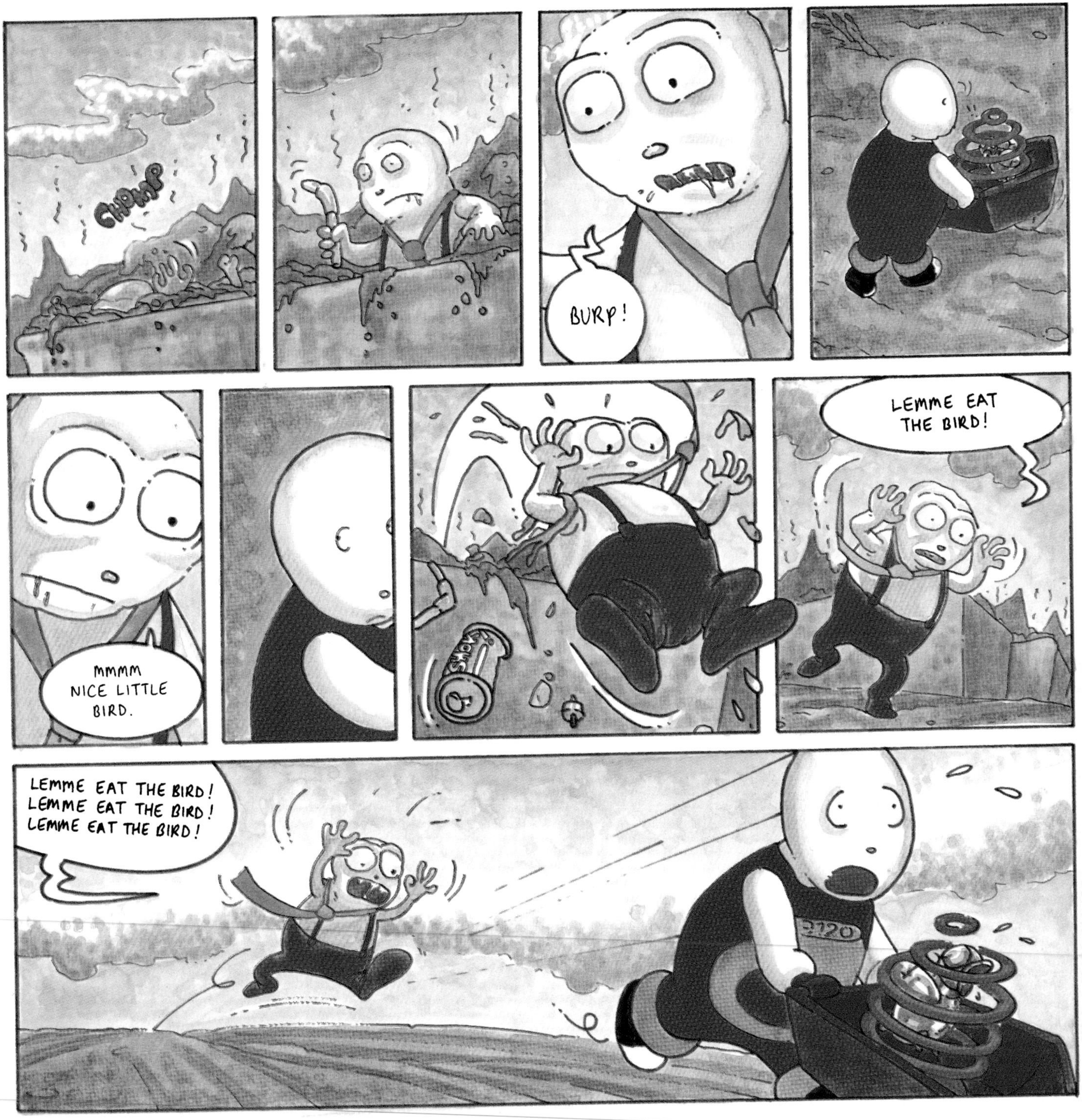
CHOMP
BURP!
MMMM
NICE LITTLE
BIRD.
LEMME EAT
THE BIRD!
LEMME EAT THE BIRD!
LEMME EAT THE BIRD!
LEMME EAT THE BIRD!

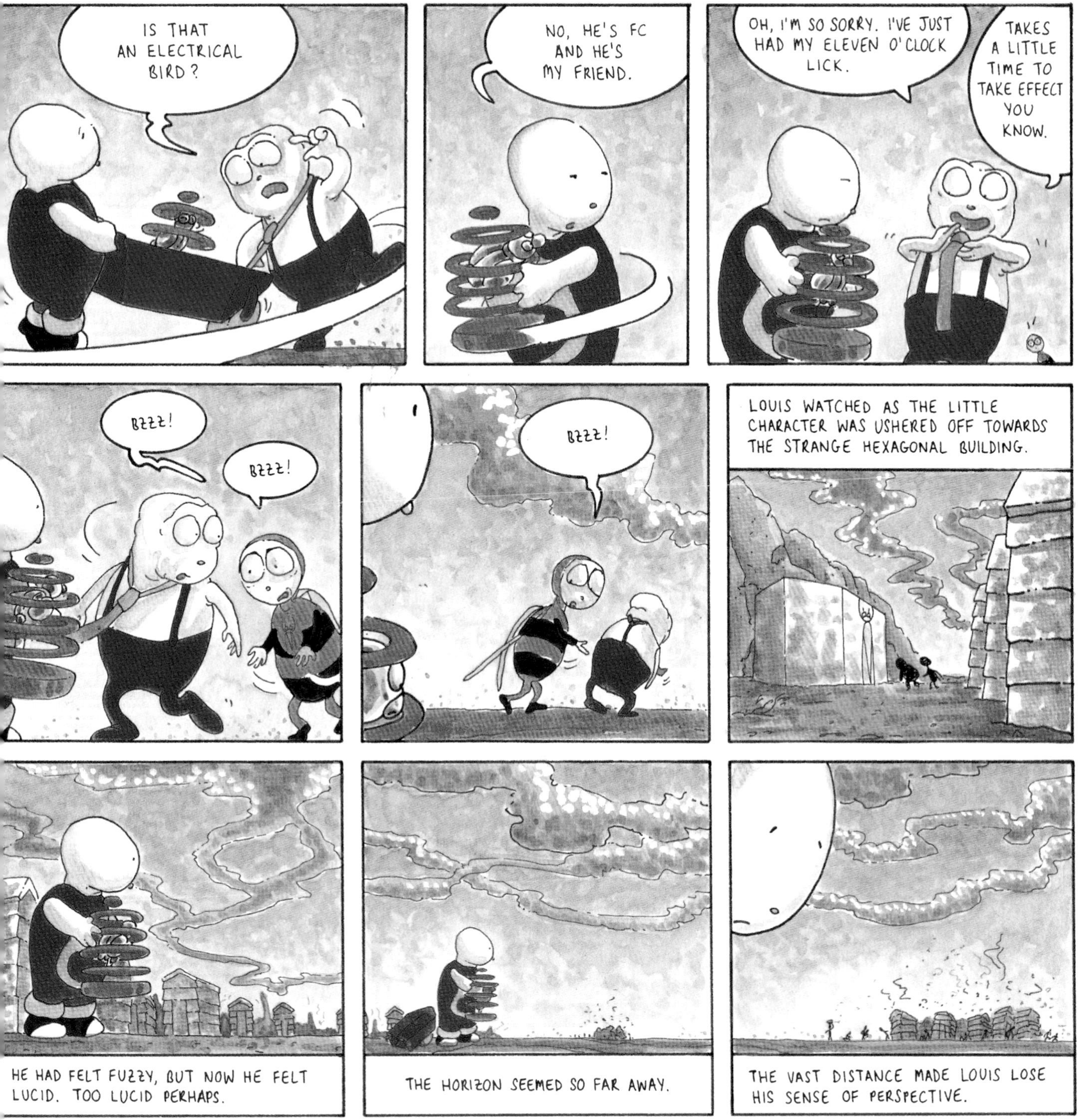
IS THAT AN ELECTRICAL BIRD?
NO, HE'S FC AND HE'S MY FRIEND.
OH, I'M SO SORRY. I'VE JUST HAD MY ELEVEN O'CLOCK LICK.
TAKES A LITTLE TIME TO TAKE EFFECT YOU KNOW.
BZZZ!
BZZZ!
BZZZ!
LOUIS WATCHED AS THE LITTLE CHARACTER WAS USHERED OFF TOWARDS THE STRANGE HEXAGONAL BUILDING.
HE HAD FELT FUZZY, BUT NOW HE FELT LUCID. TOO LUCID PERHAPS.
THE HORIZON SEEMED SO FAR AWAY.
THE VAST DISTANCE MADE LOUIS LOSE HIS SENSE OF PERSPECTIVE.

DON'T WORRY FC! LET'S GO BACK TO THE MINES.

WE'LL NEED TO BE EXTRA CAREFUL AROUND HERE!

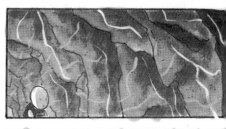

OH!

LOUIS DIDN'T LIKE TO USE THE WORD FAILURE TO DESCRIBE THE BEE FARM. IT WAS A WORD HE HAD HAD TO USE TO DESCRIBE HIMSELF, AND HIS LIFE, IN HAMLET.

HE WASN'T SURE WHERE THE WORD HAD COME FROM, OR WHAT IT REALLY MEANT.

TAC

THE WORST THING WAS, HE DID FEEL LIKE A FAILURE.

I'VE LET YOU DOWN FC.

LOUIS' FIRST IMPRESSION OF THE BEE FARM HAD BEEN UNKIND.

IT'S ME THAT'S FAILED: WHATEVER THAT MEANS.

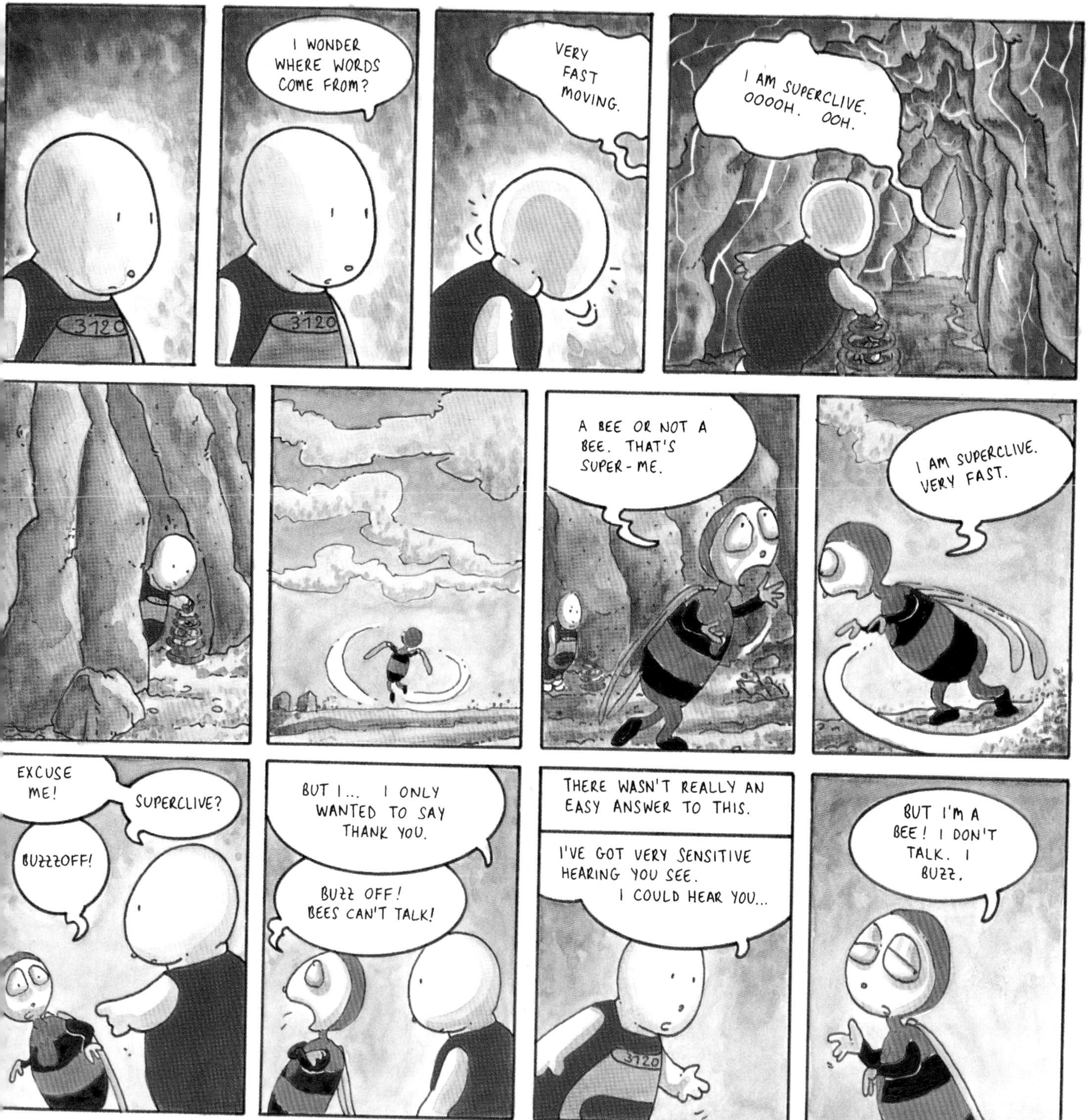
3120
I WONDER WHERE WORDS COME FROM?
3120
VERY FAST MOVING.
I AM SUPERCLIVE. OOOOH. OOH.
A BEE OR NOT A BEE. THAT'S SUPER-ME.
I AM SUPERCLIVE. VERY FAST.
EXCUSE ME!
SUPERCLIVE?
BUZZZOFF!
BUT I... I ONLY WANTED TO SAY THANK YOU.
BUZZ OFF! BEES CAN'T TALK!
THERE WASN'T REALLY AN EASY ANSWER TO THIS.
I'VE GOT VERY SENSITIVE HEARING YOU SEE. I COULD HEAR YOU...
3120
BUT I'M A BEE! I DON'T TALK. I BUZZ.

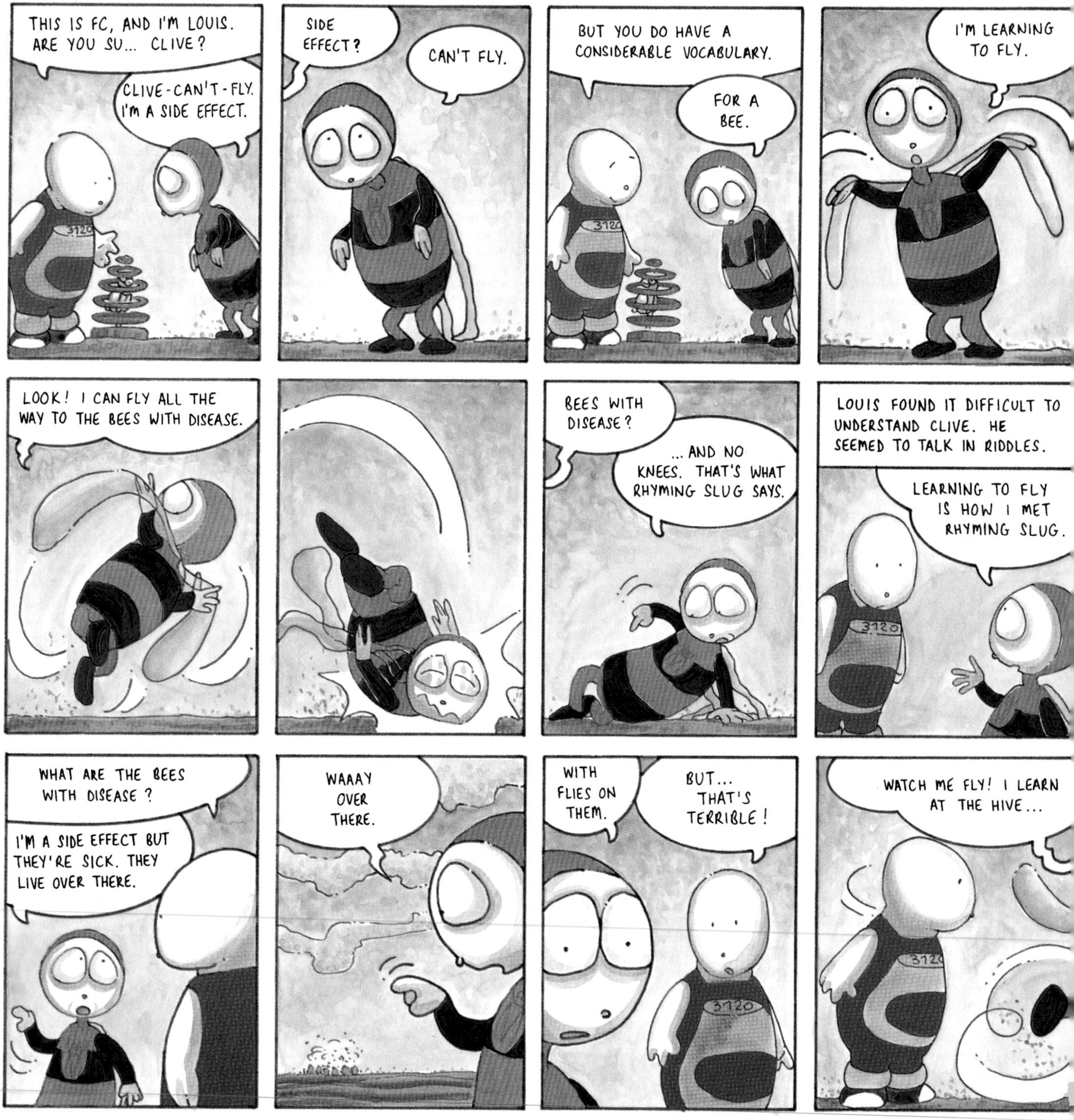
THIS IS FC, AND I'M LOUIS. ARE YOU SU... CLIVE?
CLIVE-CAN'T-FLY. I'M A SIDE EFFECT.
SIDE EFFECT?
CAN'T FLY.
BUT YOU DO HAVE A CONSIDERABLE VOCABULARY.
FOR A BEE.
I'M LEARNING TO FLY.
LOOK! I CAN FLY ALL THE WAY TO THE BEES WITH DISEASE.
BEES WITH DISEASE?
...AND NO KNEES. THAT'S WHAT RHYMING SLUG SAYS.
LOUIS FOUND IT DIFFICULT TO UNDERSTAND CLIVE. HE SEEMED TO TALK IN RIDDLES.
LEARNING TO FLY IS HOW I MET RHYMING SLUG.
WHAT ARE THE BEES WITH DISEASE?
I'M A SIDE EFFECT BUT THEY'RE SICK. THEY LIVE OVER THERE.
WAAAY OVER THERE.
WITH FLIES ON THEM.
BUT... THAT'S TERRIBLE!
WATCH ME FLY! I LEARN AT THE HIVE...

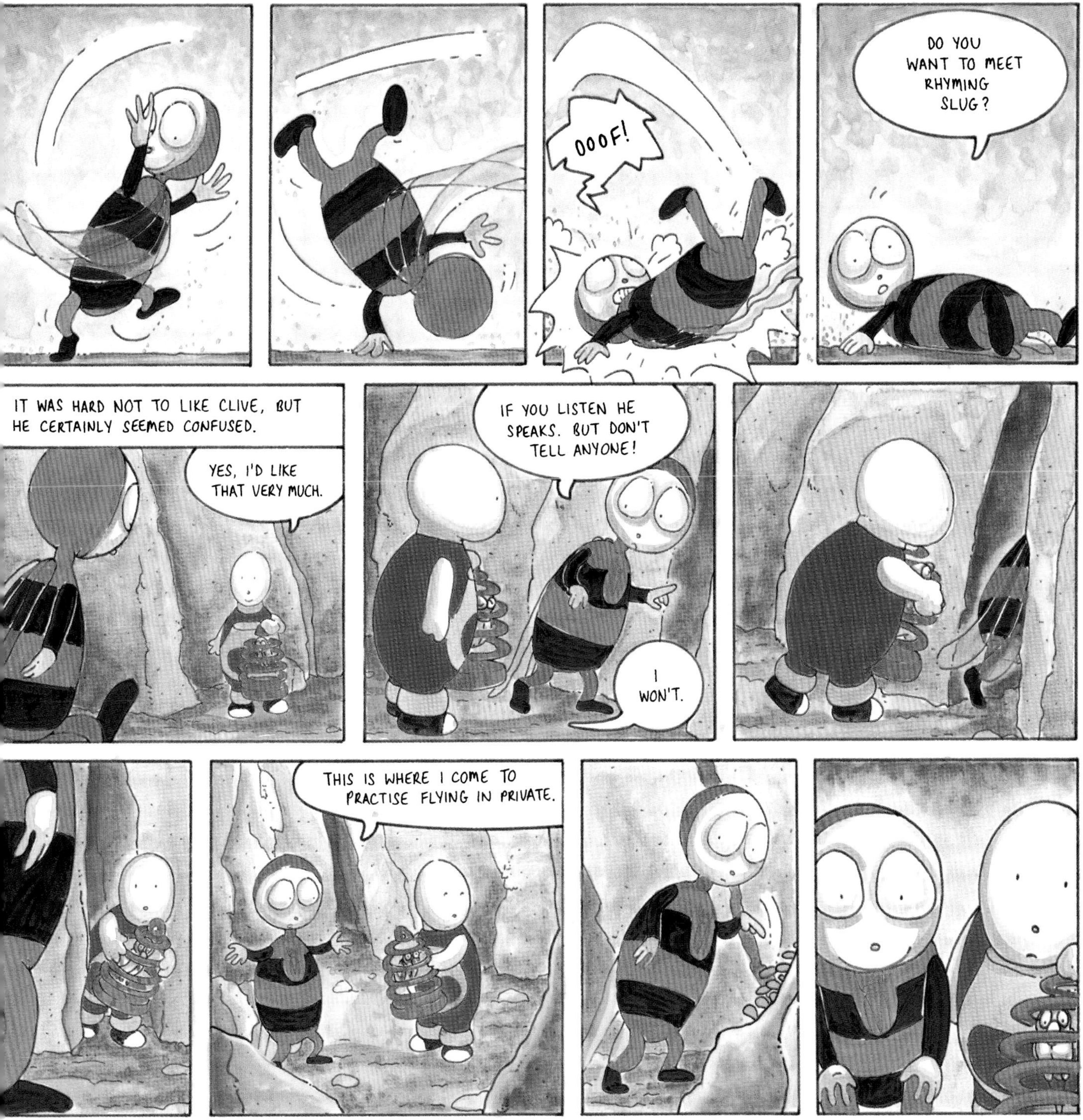

OOOF!
DO YOU WANT TO MEET RHYMING SLUG?
IT WAS HARD NOT TO LIKE CLIVE, BUT HE CERTAINLY SEEMED CONFUSED.
YES, I'D LIKE THAT VERY MUCH.
IF YOU LISTEN HE SPEAKS. BUT DON'T TELL ANYONE!
I WON'T.
THIS IS WHERE I COME TO PRACTISE FLYING IN PRIVATE.

I DON'T THINK I'VE EVER SEEN SUCH A LARGE SLUG! HAVE YOU FC?

LARGE AND GOOD VALUE.

IT MAY BE GOOD VALUE BUT IT SURE IS ITCHY.

PLEASE ASK A QUESTION.

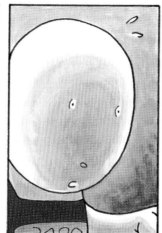

PLEASE ASK A QUESTION.

HE DOESN'T RHYME BUT IT'S A GOOD NAME ALL THE SAME. DON'T YOU THINK?

LOUIS?

OH I'M SORRY! I WAS JUST THINKING.

SOMETHING ODD...

I NAMED THE SLUG. WITH WORDS! I AM CLIVE BIG SIZE!!

Gamma Graph
NOW, MY LITTLE BEETROOTS.
AND, WHERE'S OUR NEW ARRIVAL? THE BAD EGG.
Zone 16
Zone 17
Zone 18
WHAT'S THIS??
HE DOESN'T WASTE MUCH TIME DOES HE?!! ALREADY SNOOPING IN MY SECRETS.
AND WITH ONE OF MY DRONES!!
Hub: Autharized Personnel Only !
WHICH DRONE ZONE?
AH, CLIVE.
CLIVE WILL PAY FOR THIS IN MANY LITTLE WAYS.

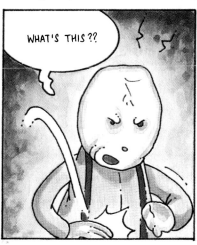

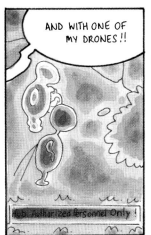

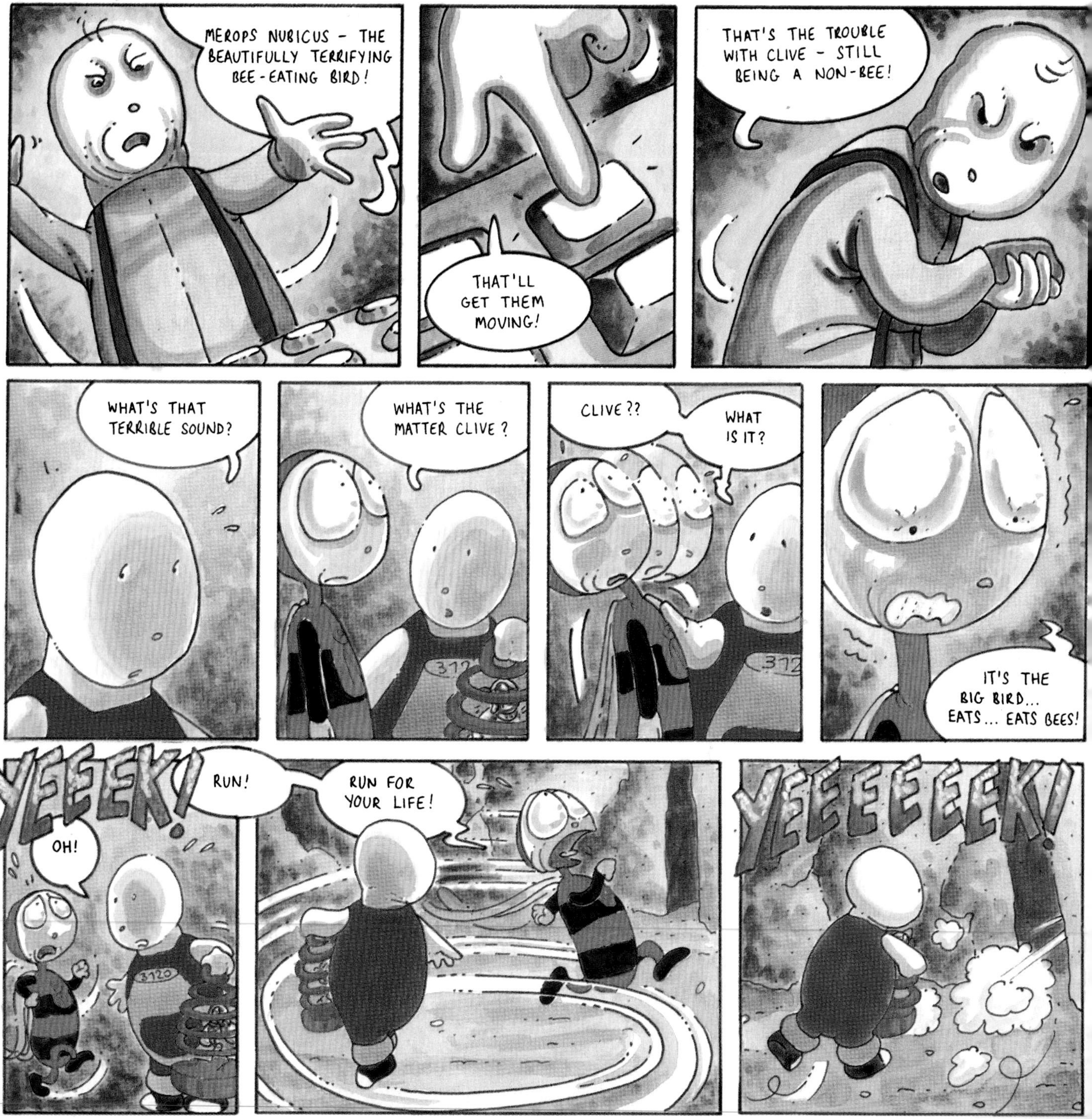
MEROPS NUBICUS - THE BEAUTIFULLY TERRIFYING BEE-EATING BIRD!
THAT'LL GET THEM MOVING!
THAT'S THE TROUBLE WITH CLIVE - STILL BEING A NON-BEE!
WHAT'S THAT TERRIBLE SOUND?
WHAT'S THE MATTER CLIVE?
CLIVE??
WHAT IS IT?
IT'S THE BIG BIRD... EATS... EATS BEES!
YEEEK!
OH!
RUN!
RUN FOR YOUR LIFE!
YEEEEEEK!

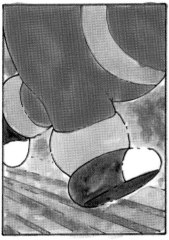

SNIP!

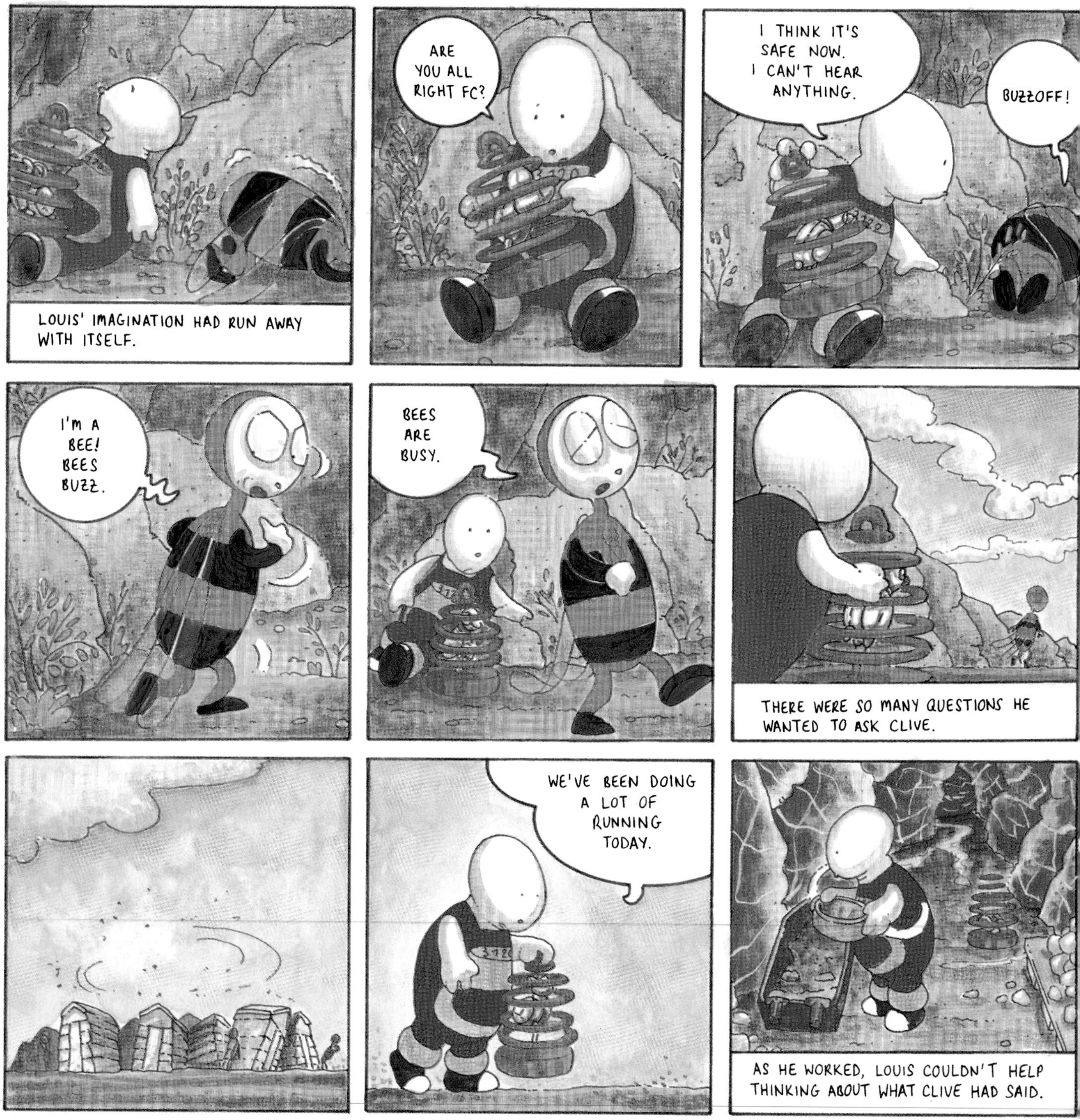
LOUIS' IMAGINATION HAD RUN AWAY WITH ITSELF.
ARE YOU ALL RIGHT FC?
I THINK IT'S SAFE NOW. I CAN'T HEAR ANYTHING.
BUZZOFF!
I'M A BEE! BEES BUZZ.
BEES ARE BUSY.
THERE WERE SO MANY QUESTIONS HE WANTED TO ASK CLIVE.
WE'VE BEEN DOING A LOT OF RUNNING TODAY.
AS HE WORKED, LOUIS COULDN'T HELP THINKING ABOUT WHAT CLIVE HAD SAID.

THE THOUGHT OF THE BEES WITH DISEASE MADE HIM FEEL MISERABLE.

HOW COULD SUCH SUFFERING BE ALLOWED?

SOMETIMES CLIVE SAYS HORRIBLE THINGS FC.

I WONDER IF HE LEARNS THEM FROM RHYMING SLUG?

MAYBE RHYMING SLUG IS LIKE CLIVE'S COMFORTER. ONLY, HE DOESN'T HAVE TO PAY.

COMFORTER

Pay Money Say Words

I SUPPOSE THAT'S BECAUSE IT COSTS CREDITS JUST TO BE HERE.

THE MORE MONETORIUM LOUIS GATHERED, THE LESS HE HAD TO PAY.

HE HAD LEARNED TO GUARD HIS PILES. THE BEE FARM WAS A DANGEROUS PLACE INDEED.

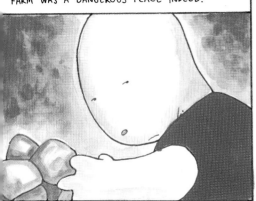

WATCH THE BIRDY!

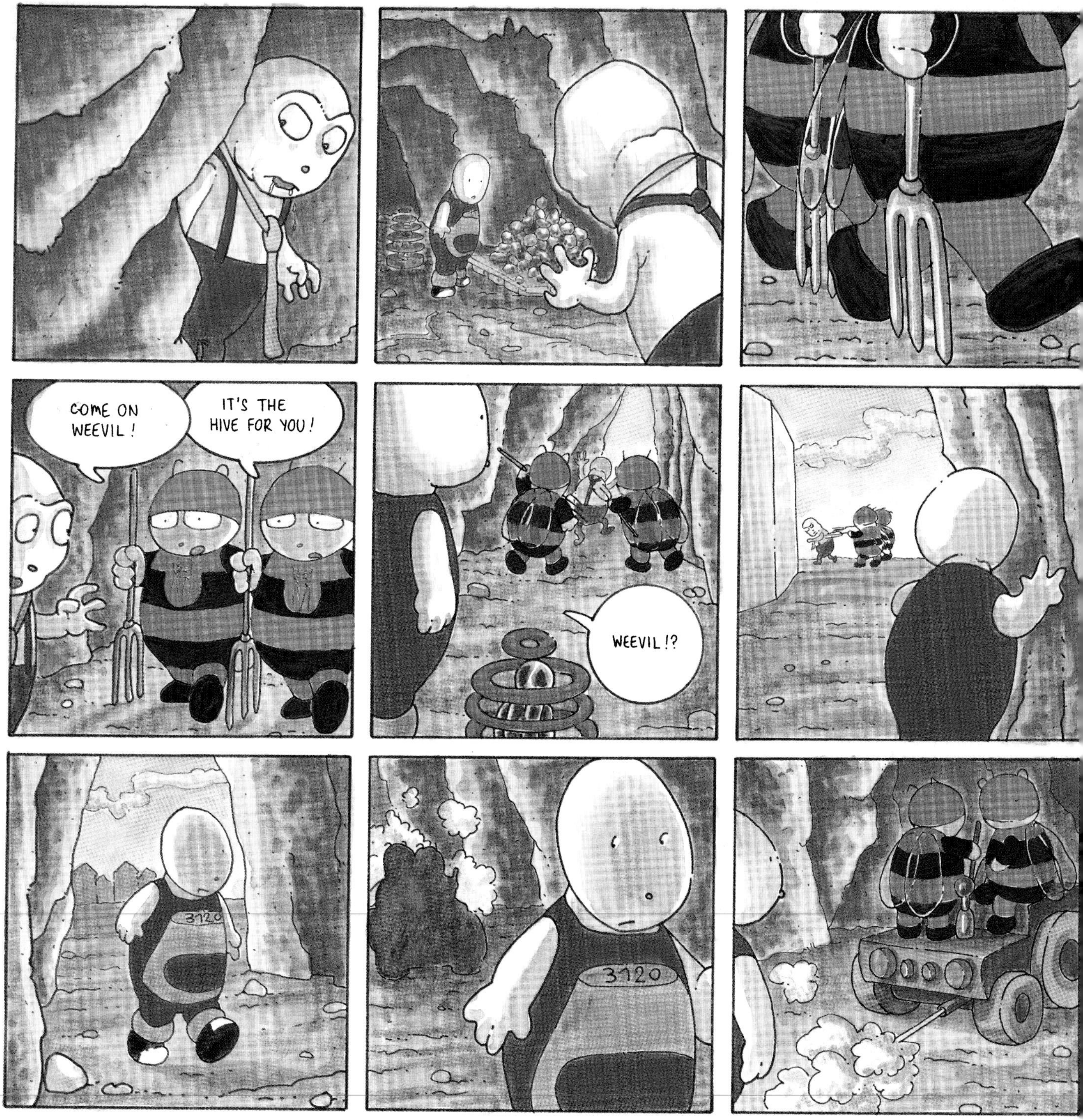
COME ON WEEVIL!
IT'S THE HIVE FOR YOU!
WEEVIL!?
3120
3120

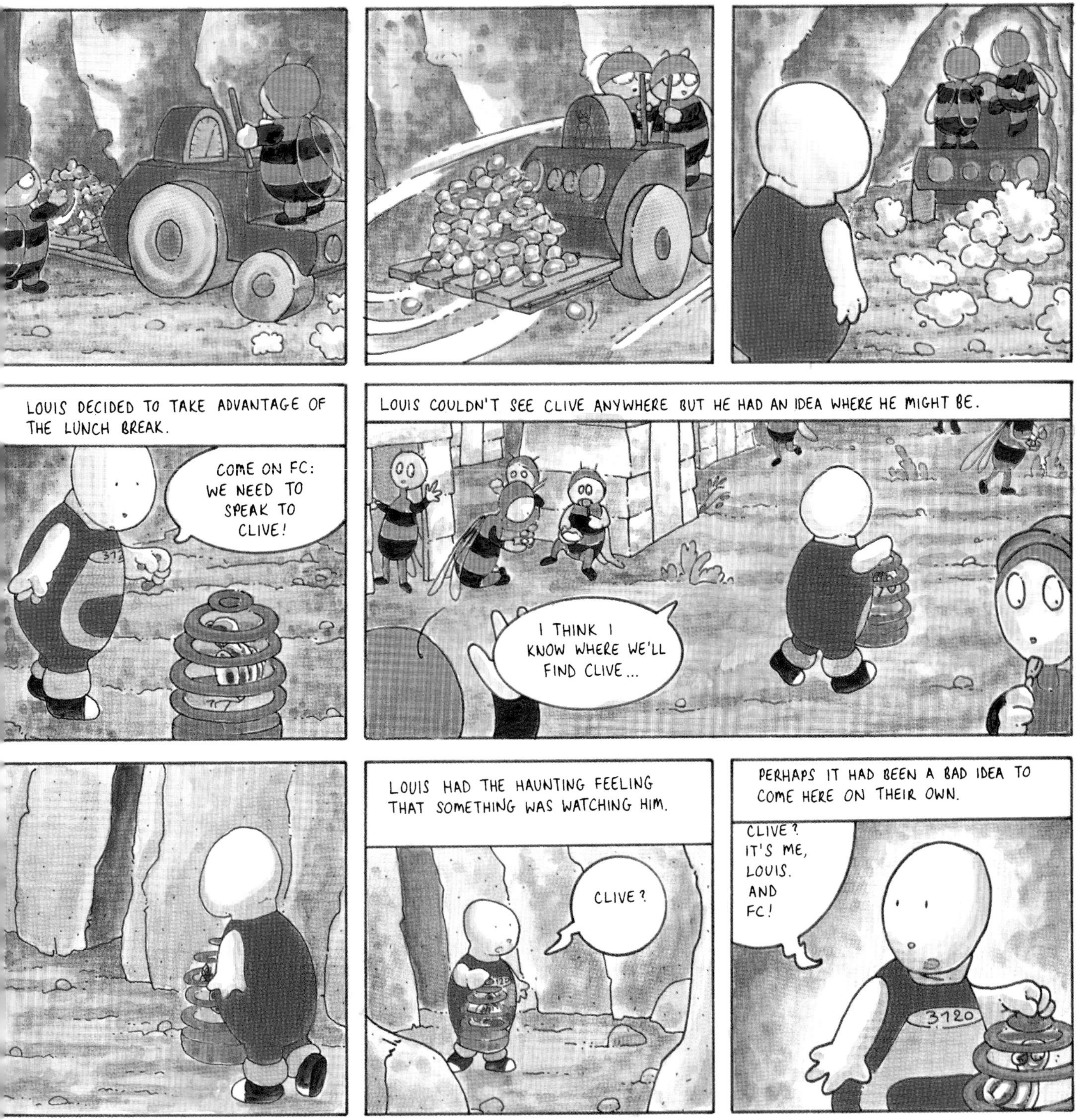

LOUIS DECIDED TO TAKE ADVANTAGE OF THE LUNCH BREAK.
COME ON FC: WE NEED TO SPEAK TO CLIVE!
LOUIS COULDN'T SEE CLIVE ANYWHERE BUT HE HAD AN IDEA WHERE HE MIGHT BE.
I THINK I KNOW WHERE WE'LL FIND CLIVE...
LOUIS HAD THE HAUNTING FEELING THAT SOMETHING WAS WATCHING HIM.
CLIVE?
PERHAPS IT HAD BEEN A BAD IDEA TO COME HERE ON THEIR OWN.
CLIVE? IT'S ME, LOUIS. AND FC!
3120

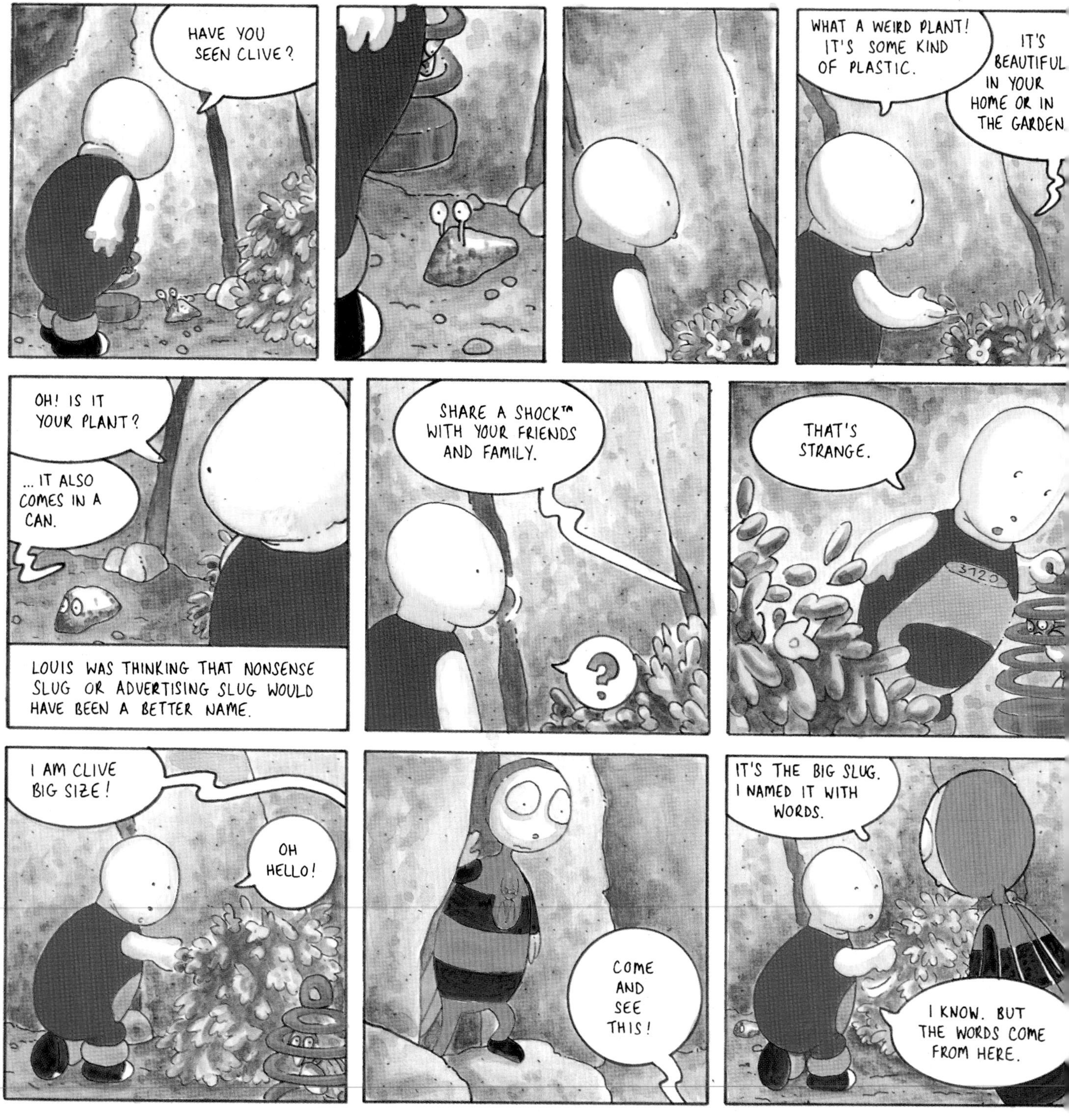
HAVE YOU SEEN CLIVE?
WHAT A WEIRD PLANT! IT'S SOME KIND OF PLASTIC.
IT'S BEAUTIFUL IN YOUR HOME OR IN THE GARDEN.
OH! IS IT YOUR PLANT?
... IT ALSO COMES IN A CAN.
LOUIS WAS THINKING THAT NONSENSE SLUG OR ADVERTISING SLUG WOULD HAVE BEEN A BETTER NAME.
SHARE A SHOCK™ WITH YOUR FRIENDS AND FAMILY.
?
THAT'S STRANGE.
3120
I AM CLIVE BIG SIZE!
OH HELLO!
COME AND SEE THIS!
IT'S THE BIG SLUG. I NAMED IT WITH WORDS.
I KNOW. BUT THE WORDS COME FROM HERE.

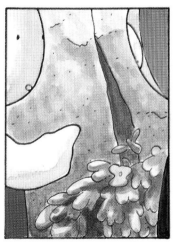

AND THIS IS AN ARTIFICIAL PLANT.

ARTIFICIAL?

PLASTIC! SNIFF IT! SMELL!

SNIFF!

IT WAS NOT EASY TO DISTINGUISH ANYTHING OVER THE BACKGROUND STINK.

WORDS GROWING FROM THE GROUND? IT'S A WORD FLOWER?

CLICK!

!!oo

IT SEEMS IMPOSSIBLE: OR AT LEAST HIGHLY UNLIKELY.

BUT IT REALLY DOES WORK.

! ?!

3120

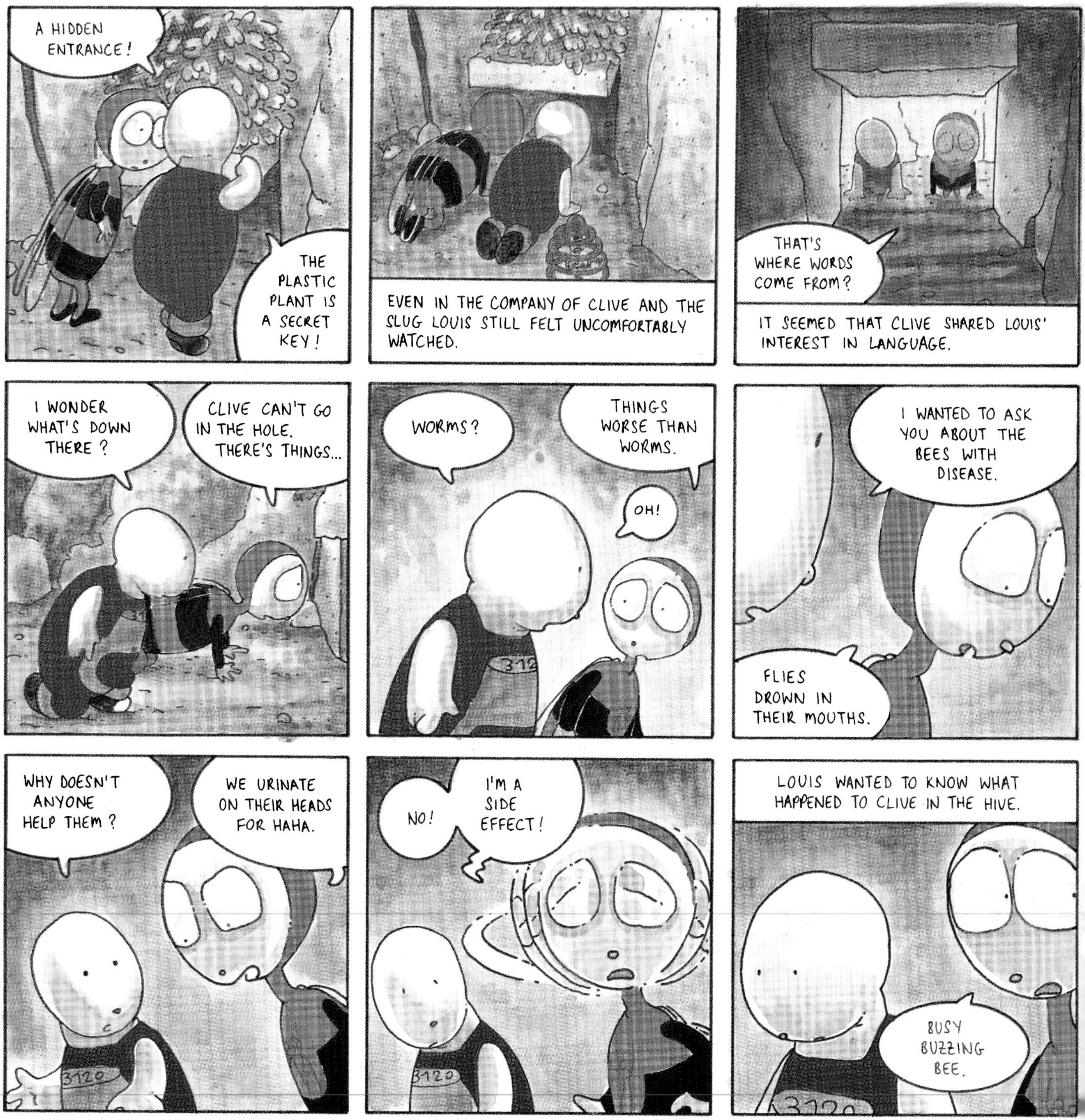
A HIDDEN ENTRANCE!
THE PLASTIC PLANT IS A SECRET KEY!
EVEN IN THE COMPANY OF CLIVE AND THE SLUG LOUIS STILL FELT UNCOMFORTABLY WATCHED.
THAT'S WHERE WORDS COME FROM?
IT SEEMED THAT CLIVE SHARED LOUIS' INTEREST IN LANGUAGE.
I WONDER WHAT'S DOWN THERE?
CLIVE CAN'T GO IN THE HOLE. THERE'S THINGS...
WORMS?
THINGS WORSE THAN WORMS.
OH!
I WANTED TO ASK YOU ABOUT THE BEES WITH DISEASE.
FLIES DROWN IN THEIR MOUTHS.
WHY DOESN'T ANYONE HELP THEM?
WE URINATE ON THEIR HEADS FOR HAHA.
NO!
I'M A SIDE EFFECT!
LOUIS WANTED TO KNOW WHAT HAPPENED TO CLIVE IN THE HIVE.
BUSY BUZZING BEE.

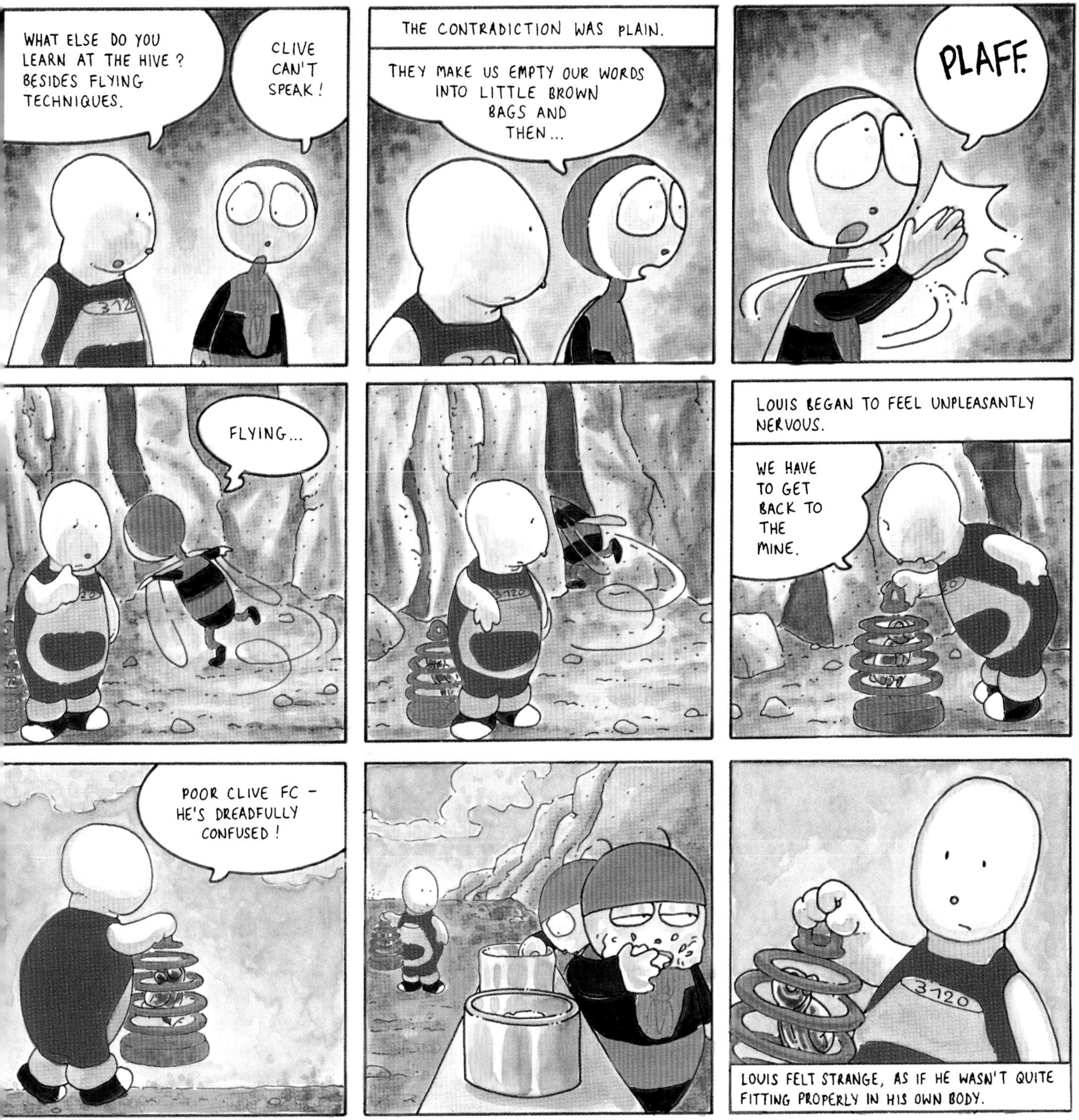
WHAT ELSE DO YOU LEARN AT THE HIVE ? BESIDES FLYING TECHNIQUES.
CLIVE CAN'T SPEAK !
THE CONTRADICTION WAS PLAIN.
THEY MAKE US EMPTY OUR WORDS INTO LITTLE BROWN BAGS AND THEN...
PLAFF.
FLYING...
LOUIS BEGAN TO FEEL UNPLEASANTLY NERVOUS.
WE HAVE TO GET BACK TO THE MINE.
POOR CLIVE FC - HE'S DREADFULLY CONFUSED !
LOUIS FELT STRANGE, AS IF HE WASN'T QUITE FITTING PROPERLY IN HIS OWN BODY.

LETTERS WERE ALLOWED, WITH A WEEKLY PICK-UP. PERHAPS WRITING TO HIS AUNT WOULD HELP LOUIS MAKE SENSE OF HIS EXPERIENCES.

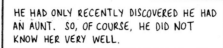

HE HAD ONLY RECENTLY DISCOVERED HE HAD AN AUNT. SO, OF COURSE, HE DID NOT KNOW HER VERY WELL.

DEAR AUNT ALISON...

LOUIS DIDN'T KNOW WHERE TO BEGIN.

IT MUST BE HARD FOR YOU TO IMAGINE A BEE FARM.

FIRST, HE GAVE HIS AUNT THE GEOGRAPHY OF THE PLACE. ITS UNIQUE FLAVOUR.

THE CONSTANT INSECT HUM.

THE ELEVEN O'CLOCK LICK AND THREE O'CLOCK SHOCK™. NOT TO MENTION LUNCH.

HE TRIED TO BRING THIS UNUSUAL WORLD ALIVE FOR HIS AUNT, WITH WORDS.

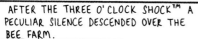
AFTER THE THREE O'CLOCK SHOCK™ A PECULIAR SILENCE DESCENDED OVER THE BEE FARM.

IT GIVES ME GAS.

HE WASN'T EVEN SURE IF HE HAD MET HIS AUNT.

QUITE AN ODD THING TO SAY. BUT LEAVING HAMLET I WAS SO UPSET.

NOTHING SEEMED REAL TO ME.

PERHAPS ALL THIS WOULD NEVER HAVE HAPPENED IF ONLY I'D CARED MORE ABOUT CREDITS.

AND NOW HERE I AM MINING THEIR VERY SUBSTANCE.

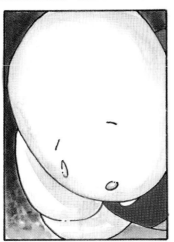

HE HAD TO TELL HIS AUNT ABOUT CLIVE.

SOMETIMES, HIS SILHOUETTE FORMS UPSIDE DOWN LETTERS AS IT JUMBLES ACROSS THE HORIZON.

LOUIS EXPLAINED WHAT THEY HAD DISCOVERED TOGETHER. AND HOW CLIVE FLED.

AFTERWARDS I FLED.

HE DESCRIBED EVERYTHING THAT HAD HAPPENED SINCE HIS ARRIVAL. A LONG DAY.

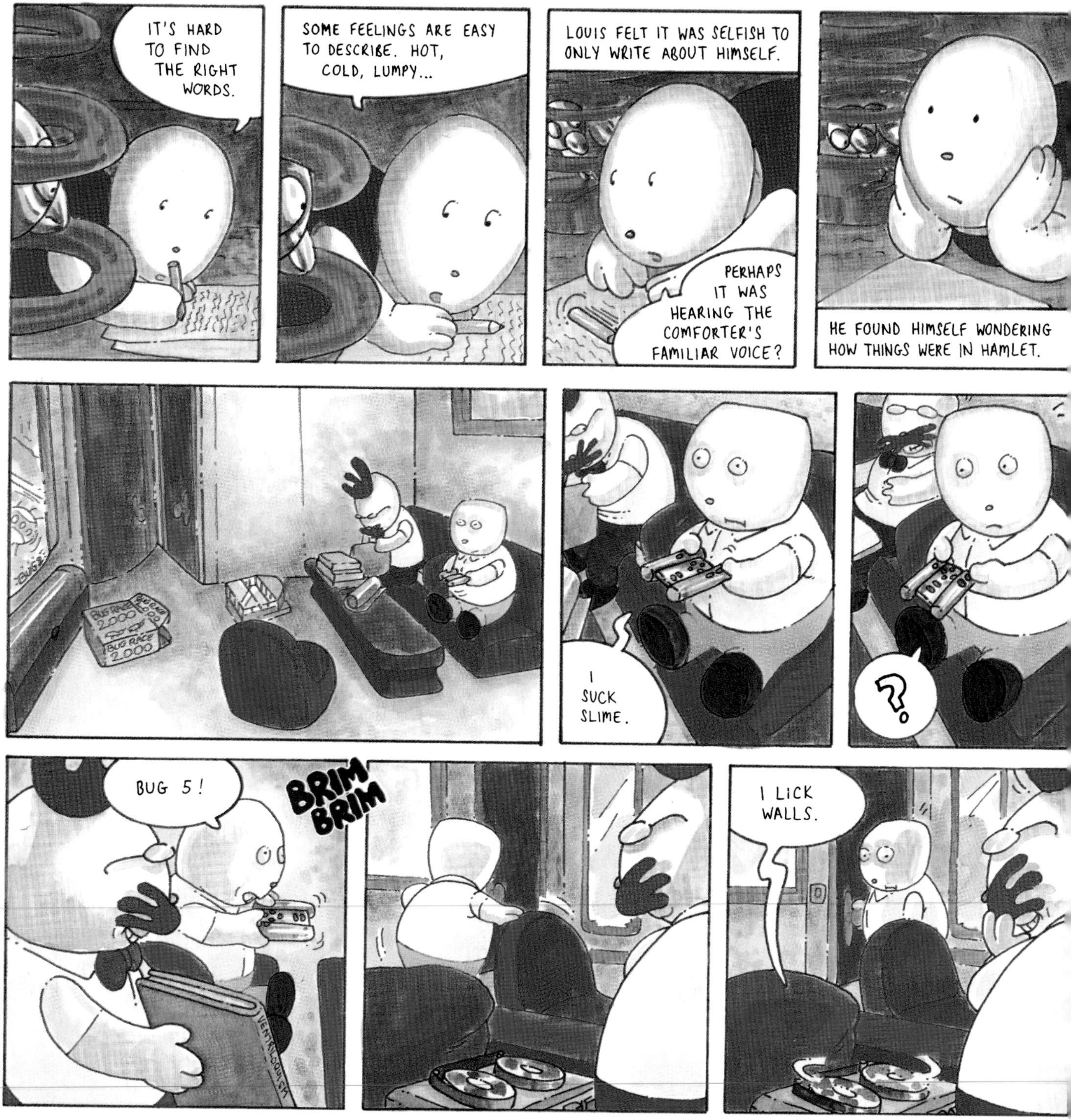
IT'S HARD TO FIND THE RIGHT WORDS.
SOME FEELINGS ARE EASY TO DESCRIBE. HOT, COLD, LUMPY...
LOUIS FELT IT WAS SELFISH TO ONLY WRITE ABOUT HIMSELF.
PERHAPS IT WAS HEARING THE COMFORTER'S FAMILIAR VOICE?
HE FOUND HIMSELF WONDERING HOW THINGS WERE IN HAMLET.
BUG RACE 2,000
BUG RACE 2,000
I SUCK SLIME.
?
BUG 5!
BRIM BRIM
VENTRILOQUISM
I LICK WALLS.

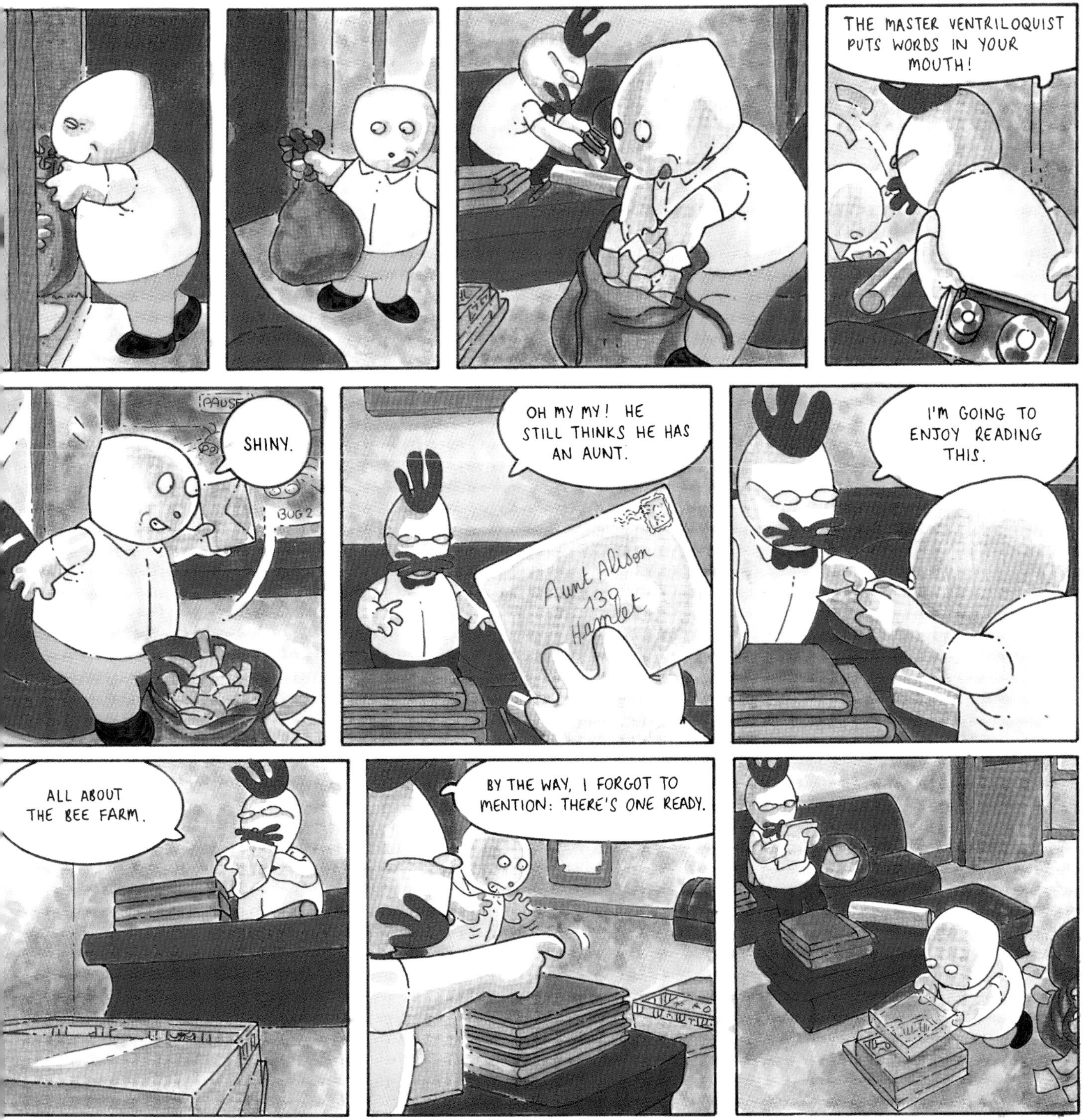
THE MASTER VENTRILOQUIST PUTS WORDS IN YOUR MOUTH!
PAUSE
SHINY.
BUG 2
OH MY MY! HE STILL THINKS HE HAS AN AUNT.
Aunt Alison
139
Hamlet
I'M GOING TO ENJOY READING THIS.
ALL ABOUT THE BEE FARM.
BY THE WAY, I FORGOT TO MENTION: THERE'S ONE READY.

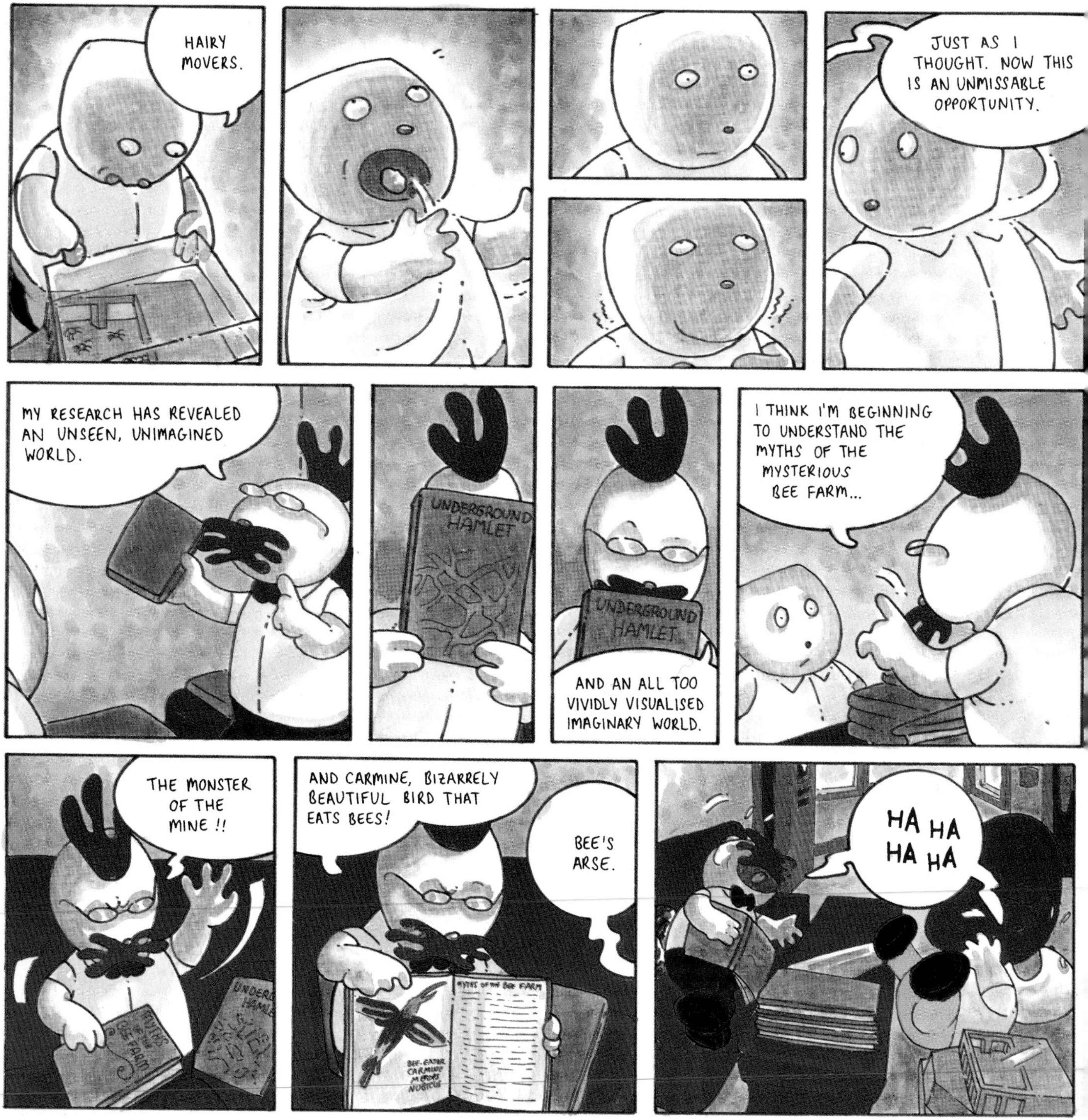
HAIRY MOVERS.
JUST AS I THOUGHT. NOW THIS IS AN UNMISSABLE OPPORTUNITY.
MY RESEARCH HAS REVEALED AN UNSEEN, UNIMAGINED WORLD.
UNDERGROUND HAMLET
UNDERGROUND HAMLET
AND AN ALL TOO VIVIDLY VISUALISED IMAGINARY WORLD.
I THINK I'M BEGINNING TO UNDERSTAND THE MYTHS OF THE MYSTERIOUS BEE FARM...
THE MONSTER OF THE MINE !!
AND CARMINE, BIZARRELY BEAUTIFUL BIRD THAT EATS BEES!
BEE'S ARSE.
MYTHS OF THE BEE FARM
BEE-EATER CARMINE MEROPS NUBICUS
HA HA HA HA

LOOK AT THIS MAP!

LIKE A GIANT RABBIT WARREN, THE OLD COMMUNICATIONS TUNNELS ARE STILL IN PLACE.

SOME ARE EVEN STILL IN USE.

WE CAN SEND A LITTLE MESSAGE TO THE BEE FARM.

KEEP LOUIS ON HIS TOES!

IT'S ALL A MATTER OF JOINING THE DOTS.

DOTS.

NOW ROAR INTO THIS MICROPHONE!

ROAR

CLIC CLIC CLIC

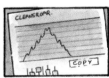

CLEANSROAR.

COPY

CLIC CLIC

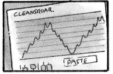

CLEANSROAR.

PASTE

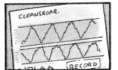

CLEANSROAR.

RECORD

39

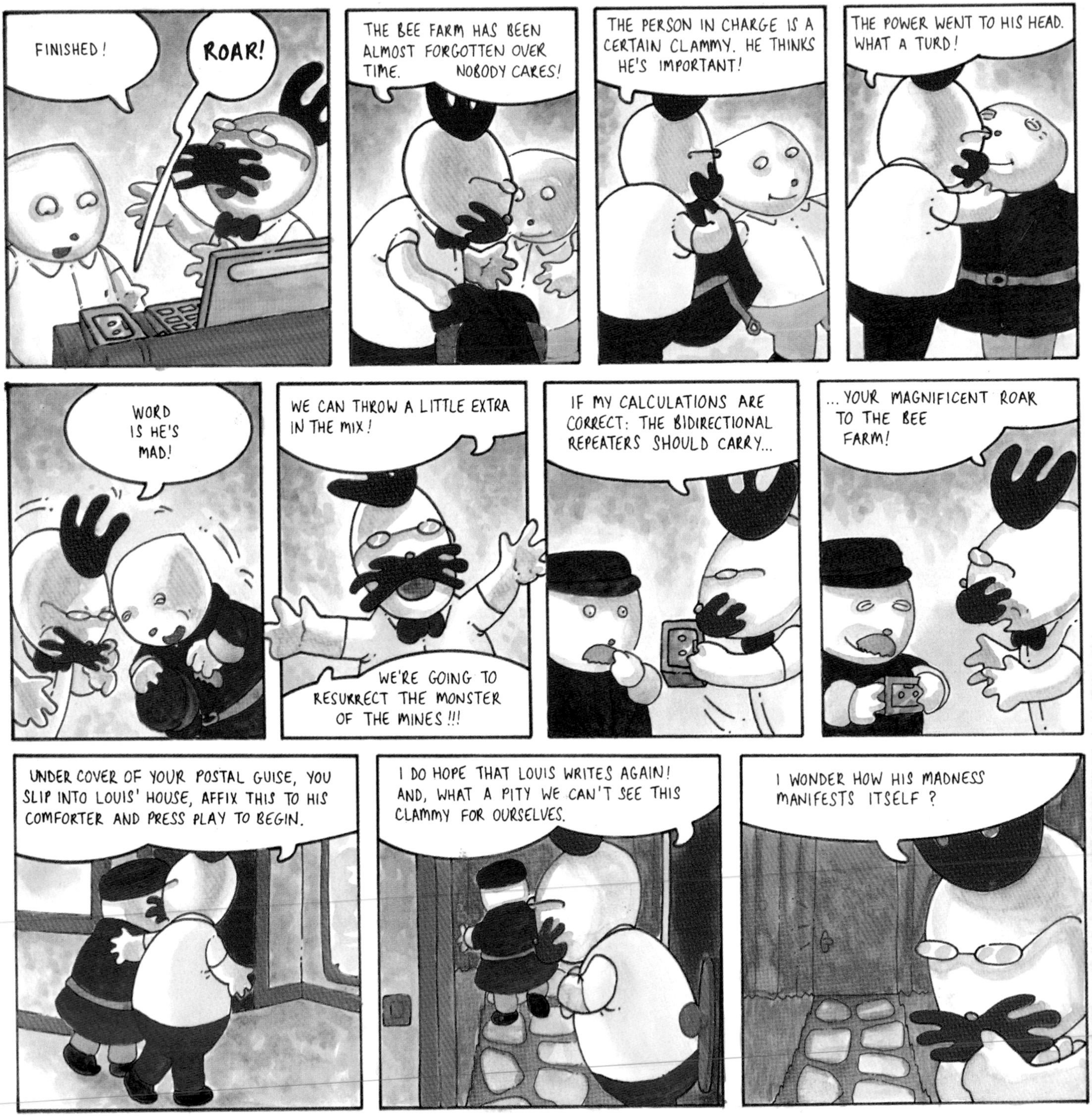
FINISHED!
ROAR!
THE BEE FARM HAS BEEN ALMOST FORGOTTEN OVER TIME. NOBODY CARES!
THE PERSON IN CHARGE IS A CERTAIN CLAMMY. HE THINKS HE'S IMPORTANT!
THE POWER WENT TO HIS HEAD. WHAT A TURD!
WORD IS HE'S MAD!
WE CAN THROW A LITTLE EXTRA IN THE MIX!
WE'RE GOING TO RESURRECT THE MONSTER OF THE MINES!!!
IF MY CALCULATIONS ARE CORRECT: THE BIDIRECTIONAL REPEATERS SHOULD CARRY...
...YOUR MAGNIFICENT ROAR TO THE BEE FARM!
UNDER COVER OF YOUR POSTAL GUISE, YOU SLIP INTO LOUIS' HOUSE, AFFIX THIS TO HIS COMFORTER AND PRESS PLAY TO BEGIN.
I DO HOPE THAT LOUIS WRITES AGAIN! AND, WHAT A PITY WE CAN'T SEE THIS CLAMMY FOR OURSELVES.
I WONDER HOW HIS MADNESS MANIFESTS ITSELF ?

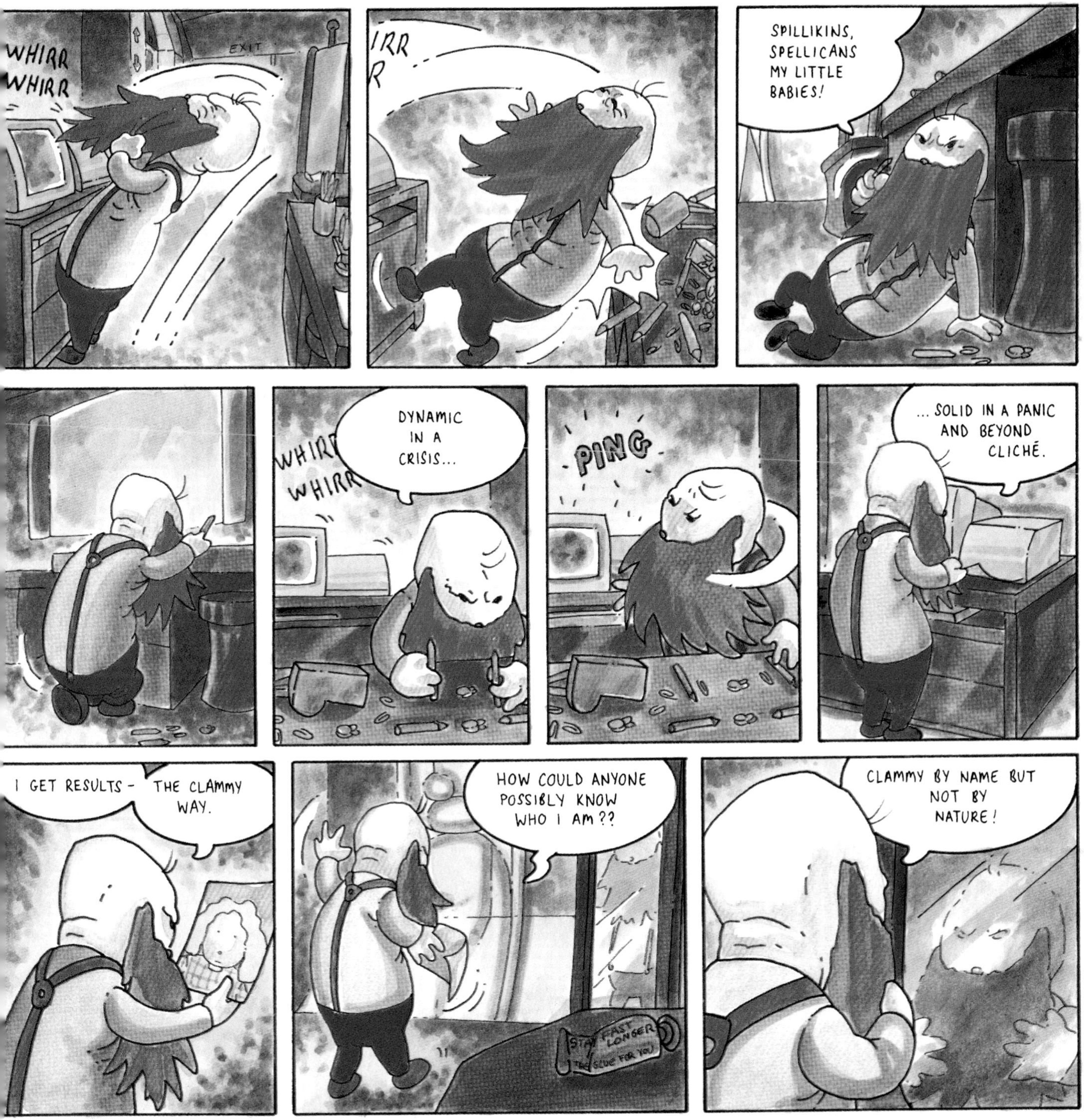
WHIRR WHIRR
EXIT
IRR R
SPILLIKINS, SPELLICANS MY LITTLE BABIES!
WHIRR WHIRR
DYNAMIC IN A CRISIS...
PING
...SOLID IN A PANIC AND BEYOND CLICHÉ.
I GET RESULTS -
THE CLAMMY WAY.
HOW COULD ANYONE POSSIBLY KNOW WHO I AM??
STAY FAST LONGER
THE GLUE FOR YOU
CLAMMY BY NAME BUT NOT BY NATURE!

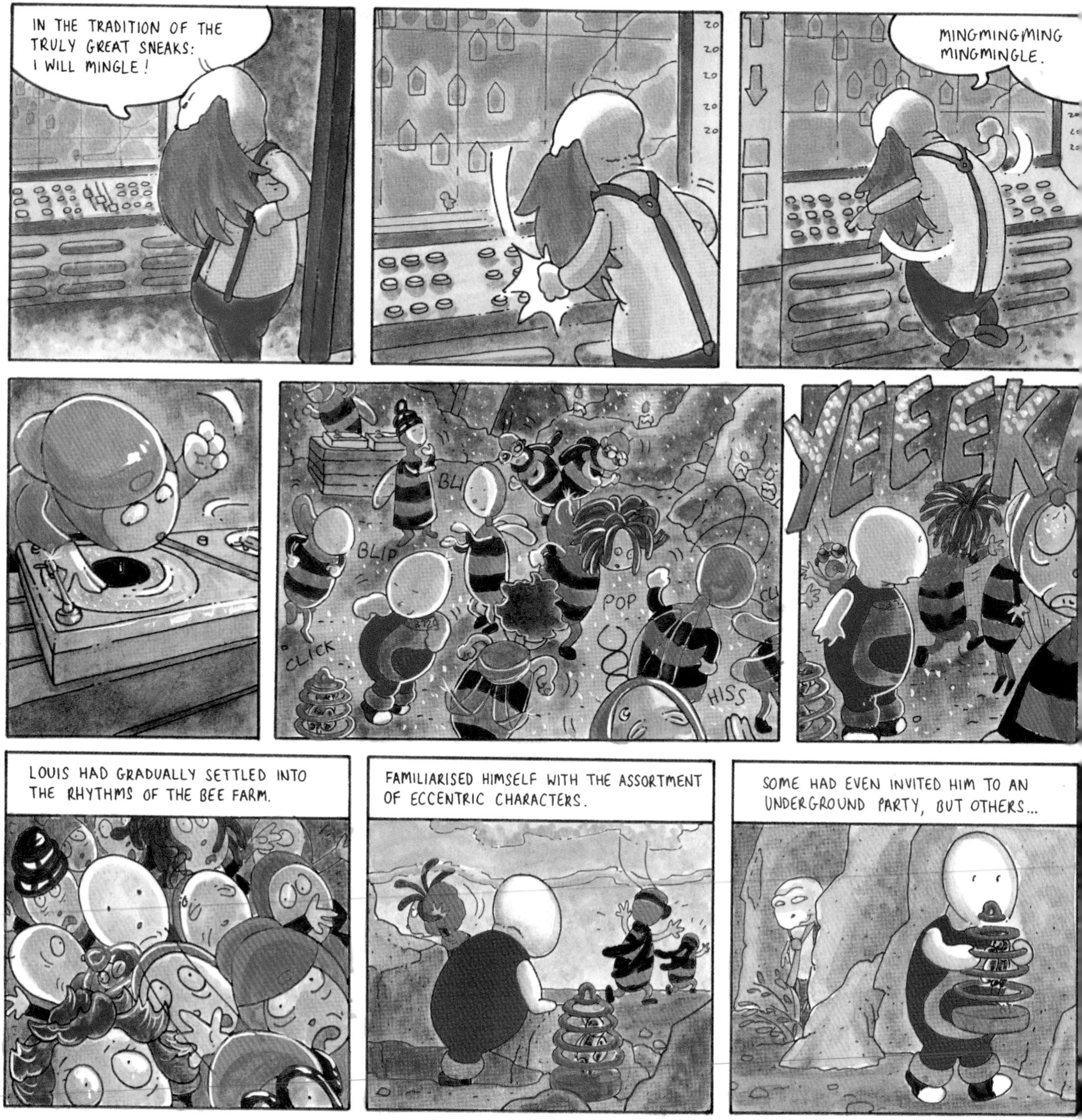

IN THE TRADITION OF THE TRULY GREAT SNEAKS: I WILL MINGLE!
MINGMINGMING MINGMINGLE.
BLIP
BLIP
POP
CLICK
HISS
YEEEK
LOUIS HAD GRADUALLY SETTLED INTO THE RHYTHMS OF THE BEE FARM.
FAMILIARISED HIMSELF WITH THE ASSORTMENT OF ECCENTRIC CHARACTERS.
SOME HAD EVEN INVITED HIM TO AN UNDERGROUND PARTY, BUT OTHERS...

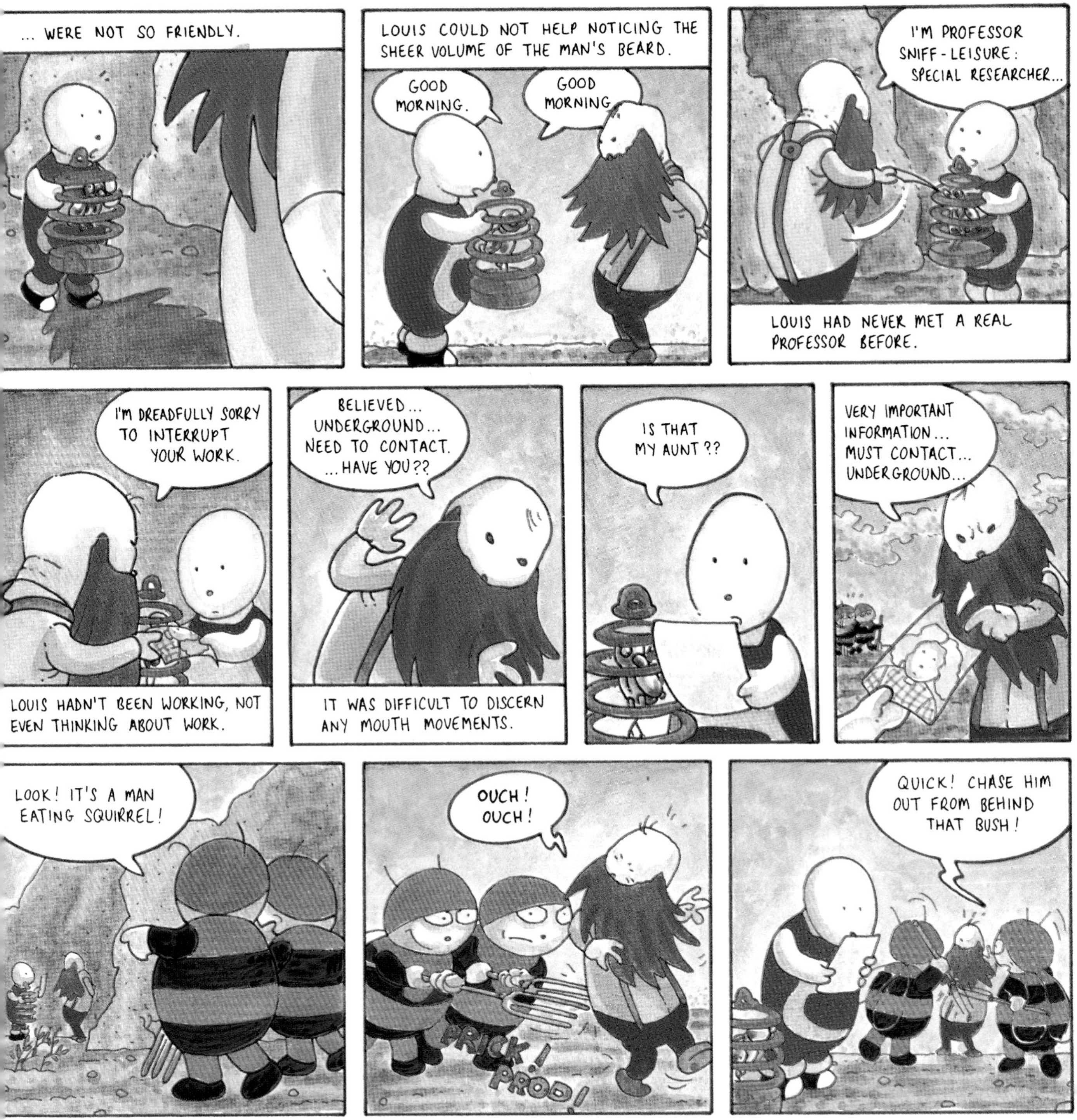
... WERE NOT SO FRIENDLY.
LOUIS COULD NOT HELP NOTICING THE SHEER VOLUME OF THE MAN'S BEARD.
GOOD MORNING.
GOOD MORNING.
I'M PROFESSOR SNIFF-LEISURE: SPECIAL RESEARCHER...
LOUIS HAD NEVER MET A REAL PROFESSOR BEFORE.
I'M DREADFULLY SORRY TO INTERRUPT YOUR WORK.
LOUIS HADN'T BEEN WORKING, NOT EVEN THINKING ABOUT WORK.
BELIEVED... UNDERGROUND... NEED TO CONTACT. ...HAVE YOU??
IT WAS DIFFICULT TO DISCERN ANY MOUTH MOVEMENTS.
IS THAT MY AUNT??
VERY IMPORTANT INFORMATION... MUST CONTACT... UNDERGROUND...
LOOK! IT'S A MAN EATING SQUIRREL!
OUCH! OUCH!
PRICK! PROD!
QUICK! CHASE HIM OUT FROM BEHIND THAT BUSH!

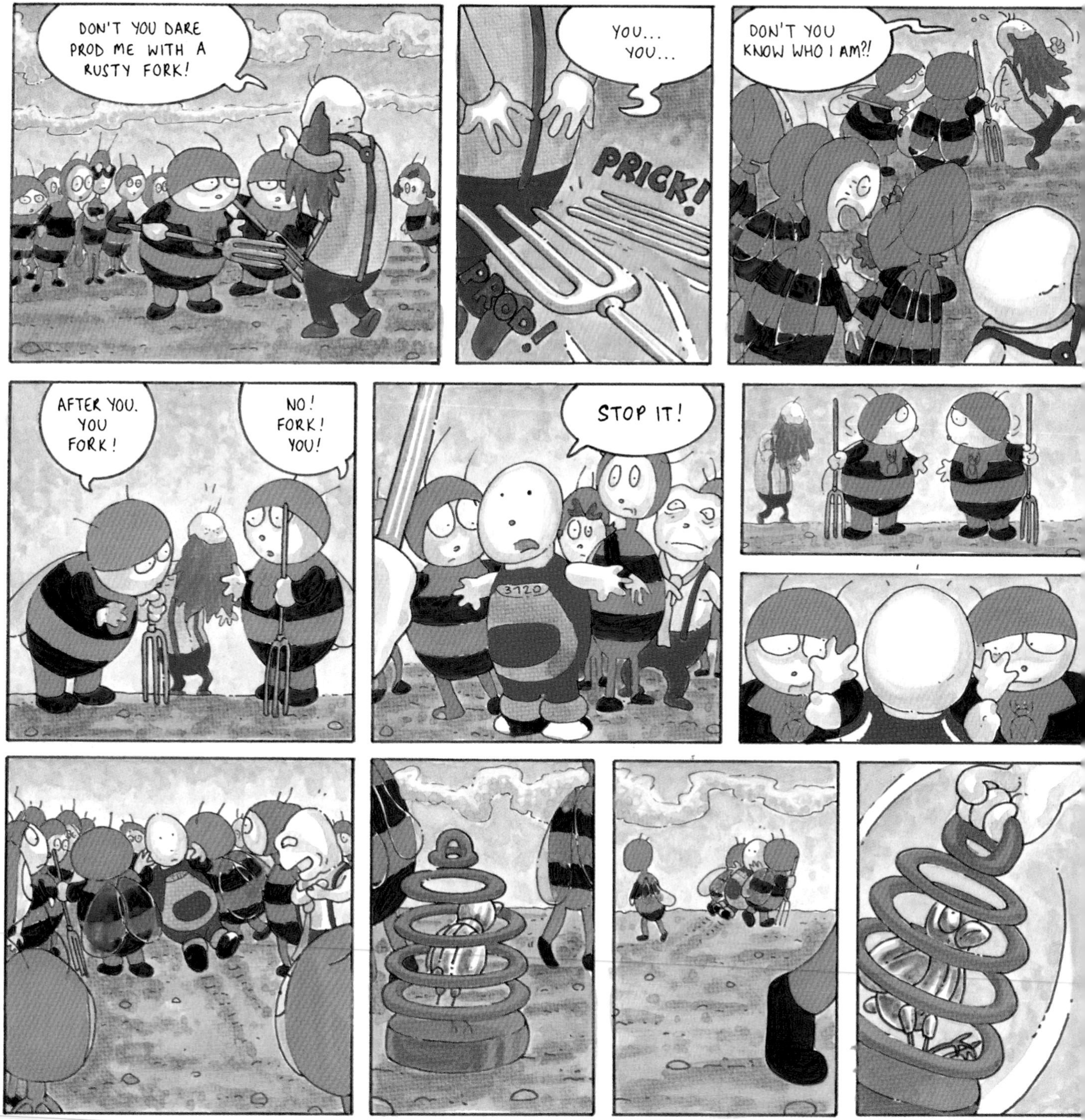

DON'T YOU DARE PROD ME WITH A RUSTY FORK!
YOU... YOU...
PRICK!
PROD!
DON'T YOU KNOW WHO I AM?!
AFTER YOU. YOU FORK!
NO! FORK! YOU!
STOP IT!
3120

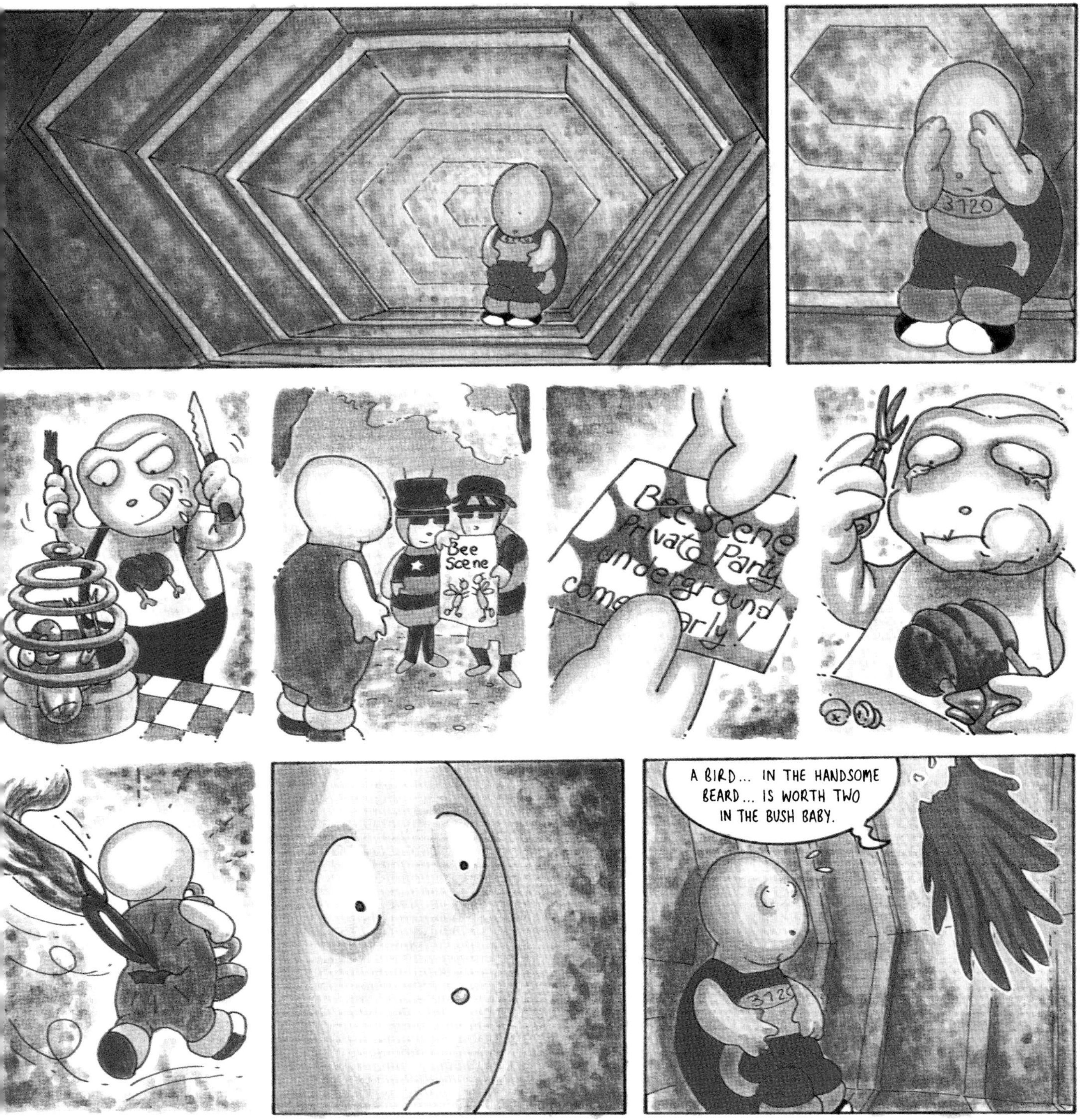
3720
Bee Scene
Bee Scene
Private Party
underground
A BIRD... IN THE HANDSOME BEARD... IS WORTH TWO IN THE BUSH BABY.
3720

IT DIDN'T MAKE MUCH SENSE.

AND, WHAT WOULD THE PROFESSOR BE DOING WITH A PICTURE OF MY AUNT?

WHAT DID I GO AND DO THAT FOR?

NOW HE'S WEEVIL FOOD!

THOSE DRONES CERTAINLY HAD NO TROUBLE TALKING!

HE THOUGHT OF CLIVE; OF CLIVE'S CONFUSION. THE THINGS HE SAID.

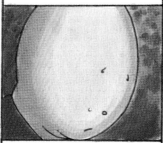

WHAT REALLY HAPPENED HERE INSIDE THE HIVE?

HIS THOUGHTS TURNED, ONCE MORE, TO THE BEES WITH DISEASE.

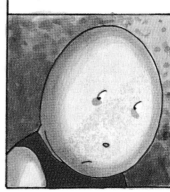

THE SUFFERING. THE FLIES THAT DROWNED IN THEIR MOUTHS.

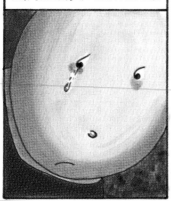

THERE WERE PLENTY OF FLIES HERE, ON THE BEE FARM. ESPECIALLY AFTER WORKING HARD.

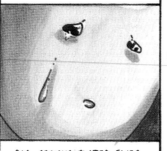

BIG, ARMOUR-PLATED FLIES.

LOUIS WISHED HE WOULD DROWN IN HIS OWN TEARS.

HIS BODY GREW TIRED AND HEAVY.

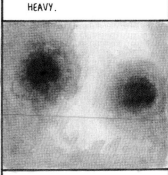

THEN HE STOPPED BEING ABLE TO SENSE IT AT ALL...

NNNNNNNN.

"IS THAT MY AUNT?"

AND THEN HE DARES "RESCUE ME" FROM MY OWN DRONES.

WELL... I DON'T CARE ABOUT GATHERING INTELLIGENCE... I'VE GOT OTHER WAYS TO IMPRESS...

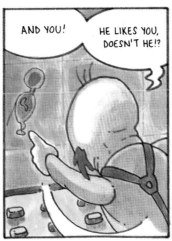

AND YOU!

HE LIKES YOU, DOESN'T HE!?

AND THAT GIVES ME AN IDEA.

SOMETHING NEW, I THINK!

GET ME DRONE CLIVE TO THE HIVE!

EXIT

IF HE'S SO INTERESTED IN THE TUNNEL SYSTEM, HE CAN CRAWL DOWN...

CREEPY CRAWLS: DOWN DOWN DOWN...

COME WITH ME ON A JOURNEY INTO GROUND...

THE TUNNEL IS DARK AND FILLED WITH FEAR. BUT YOU MUST GO ON, THE END IS NEAR...

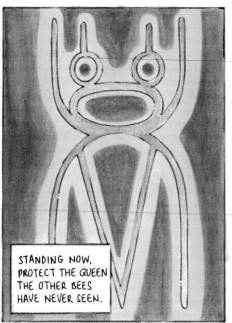

STANDING NOW, PROTECT THE QUEEN THE OTHER BEES HAVE NEVER SEEN.

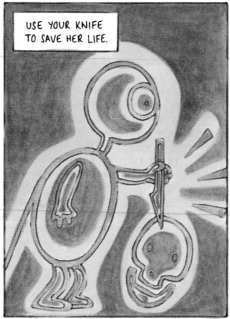

USE YOUR KNIFE TO SAVE HER LIFE.

NEW FRIEND CLIVE BECOMES...

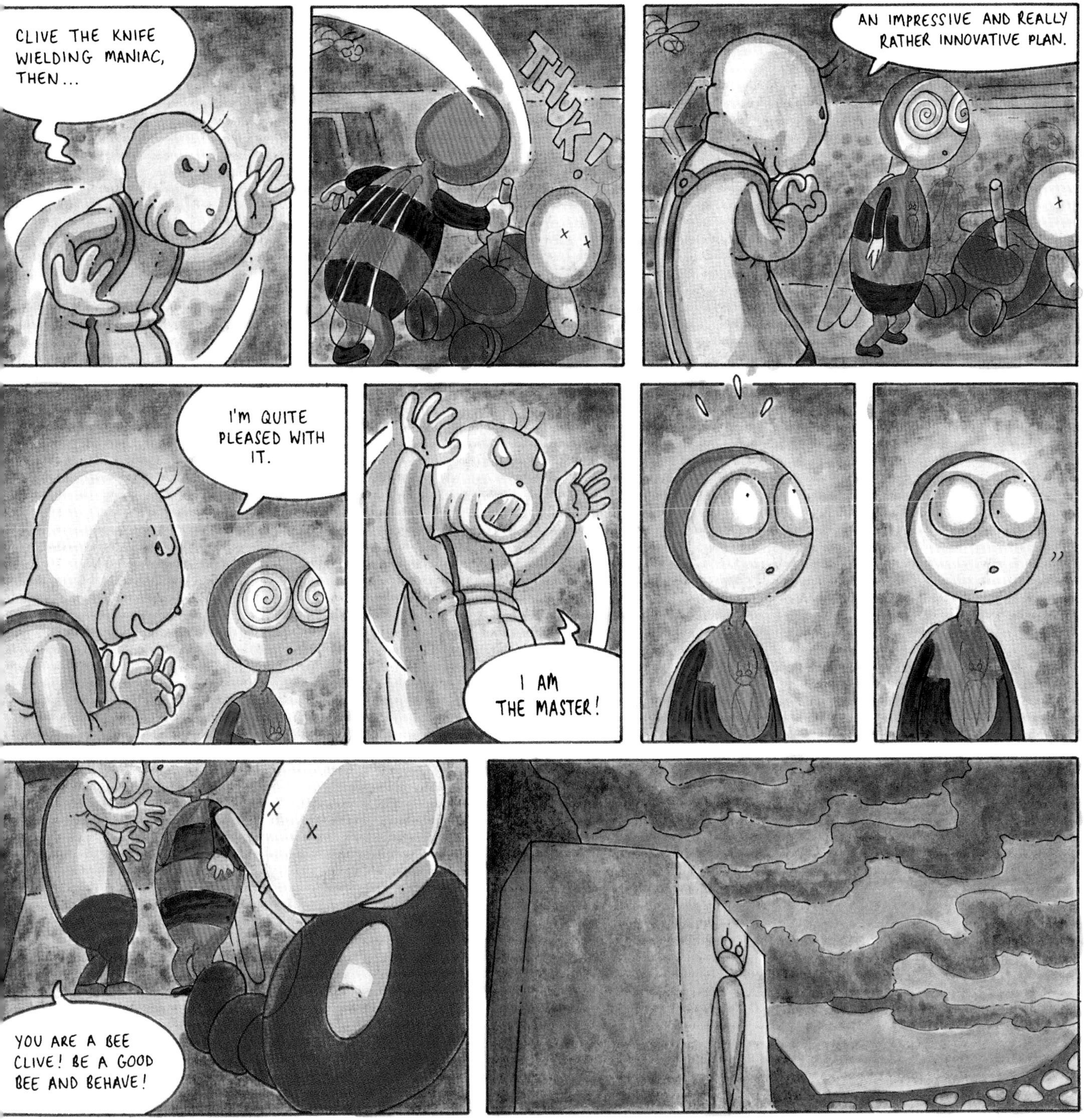
CLIVE THE KNIFE WIELDING MANIAC, THEN...
THUK!
AN IMPRESSIVE AND REALLY RATHER INNOVATIVE PLAN.
I'M QUITE PLEASED WITH IT.
I AM THE MASTER!
YOU ARE A BEE CLIVE! BE A GOOD BEE AND BEHAVE!

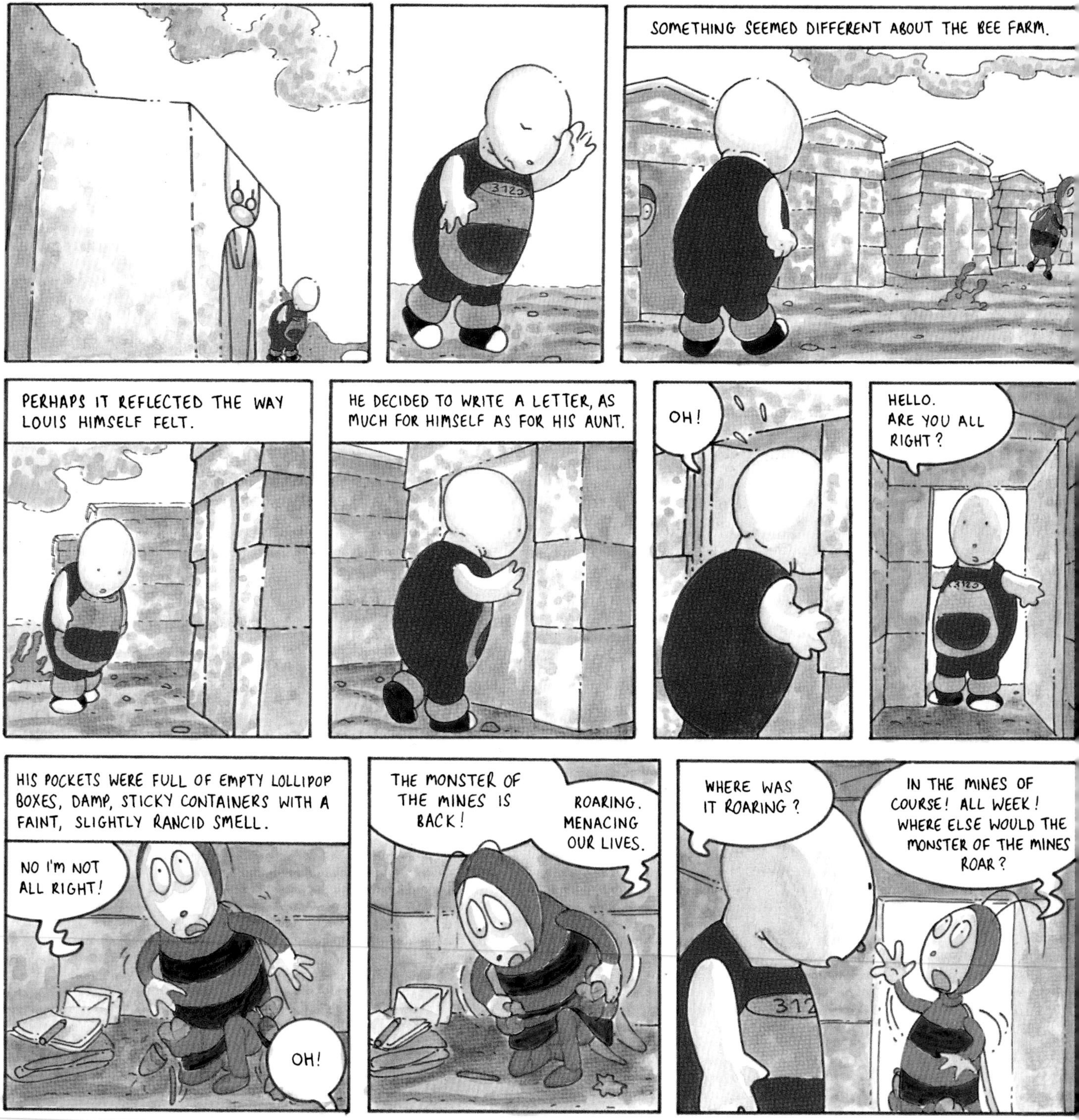
SOMETHING SEEMED DIFFERENT ABOUT THE BEE FARM.
PERHAPS IT REFLECTED THE WAY LOUIS HIMSELF FELT.
HE DECIDED TO WRITE A LETTER, AS MUCH FOR HIMSELF AS FOR HIS AUNT.
OH!
HELLO. ARE YOU ALL RIGHT?
HIS POCKETS WERE FULL OF EMPTY LOLLIPOP BOXES, DAMP, STICKY CONTAINERS WITH A FAINT, SLIGHTLY RANCID SMELL.
NO I'M NOT ALL RIGHT!
OH!
THE MONSTER OF THE MINES IS BACK!
ROARING. MENACING OUR LIVES.
WHERE WAS IT ROARING?
IN THE MINES OF COURSE! ALL WEEK! WHERE ELSE WOULD THE MONSTER OF THE MINES ROAR?

HOW COULD ANYONE POSSIBLY BE ALL RIGHT??

AS HE RELATED THESE EVENTS TO HIS AUNT HE REFLECTED ON THE MONSTER.

ROARING FROM THE MINES HAS MADE THE BEE FARM A FRIGHTENED PLACE.

OUR TRANSMISSION ACCOMPLISHED.

VENTRILOQUISM FOR EXPERTS!

A WONDERFUL MIXTURE OF MODERN TECHNOLOGY AND PLAIN OLD SUPERSTITION.

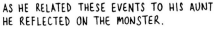

WHAT ELSE DOES LOUIS HAVE TO SAY?

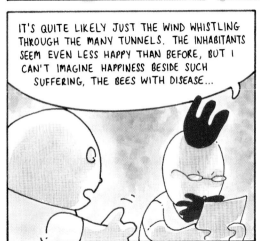

IT'S QUITE LIKELY JUST THE WIND WHISTLING THROUGH THE MANY TUNNELS. THE INHABITANTS SEEM EVEN LESS HAPPY THAN BEFORE, BUT I CAN'T IMAGINE HAPPINESS BESIDE SUCH SUFFERING, THE BEES WITH DISEASE...

I'LL GIVE HIM WIND IN TUNNELS!

BUT, SINCE I LOST FC, MY HEART IS BROKEN. I NO LONGER CARE WHAT HAPPENS TO ME: I AM THE MONSTER.

OH THAT'S GOOD: I AM THE MONSTER!

I AM THE MONSTAH!!

I THINK WE MUST MODIFY OUR BROADCAST.

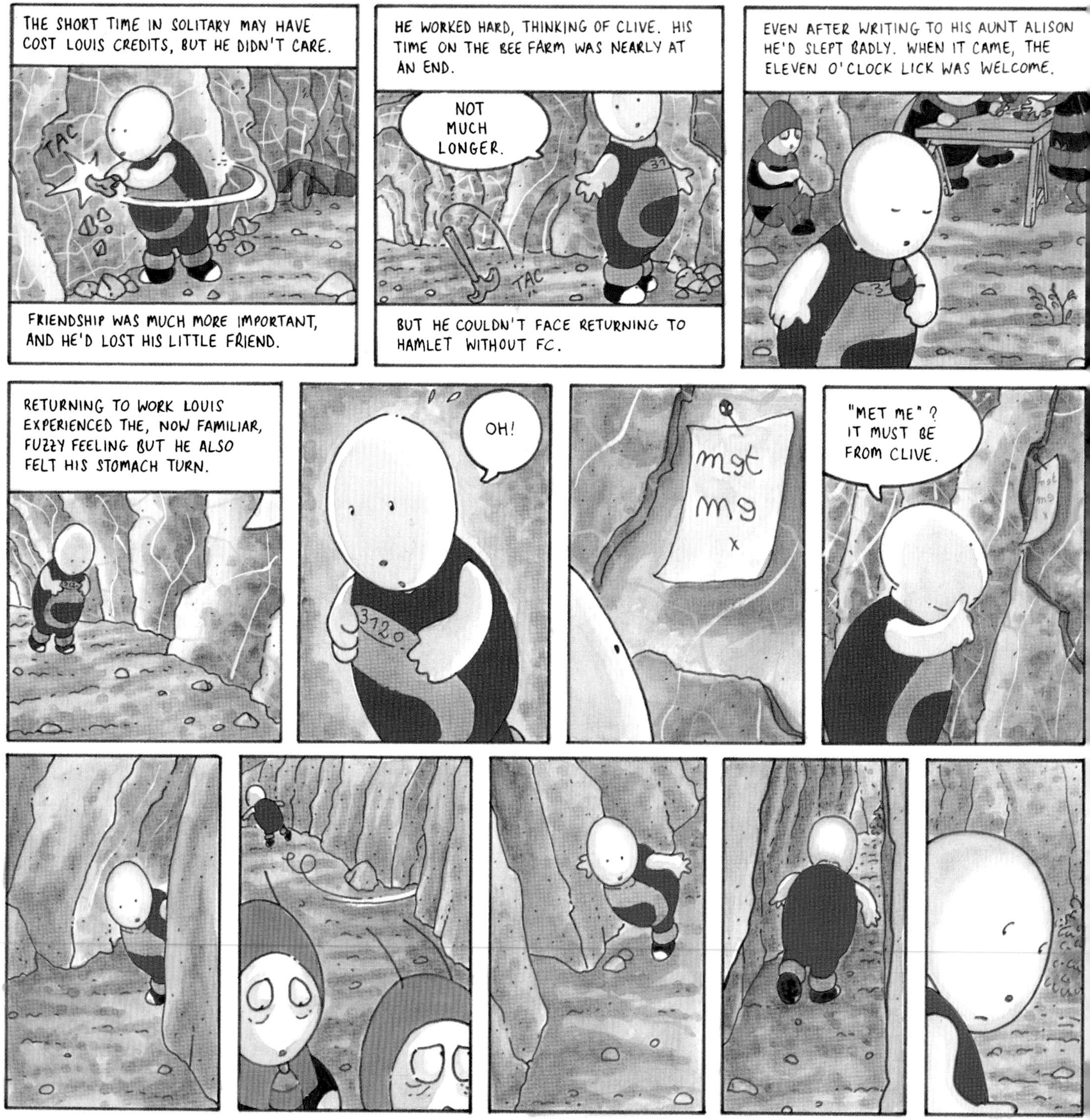
THE SHORT TIME IN SOLITARY MAY HAVE COST LOUIS CREDITS, BUT HE DIDN'T CARE.
TAC
FRIENDSHIP WAS MUCH MORE IMPORTANT, AND HE'D LOST HIS LITTLE FRIEND.
HE WORKED HARD, THINKING OF CLIVE. HIS TIME ON THE BEE FARM WAS NEARLY AT AN END.
NOT MUCH LONGER.
TAC
BUT HE COULDN'T FACE RETURNING TO HAMLET WITHOUT FC.
EVEN AFTER WRITING TO HIS AUNT ALISON HE'D SLEPT BADLY. WHEN IT CAME, THE ELEVEN O'CLOCK LICK WAS WELCOME.
RETURNING TO WORK LOUIS EXPERIENCED THE, NOW FAMILIAR, FUZZY FEELING BUT HE ALSO FELT HIS STOMACH TURN.
OH!
3120
mgt mg
x
"MET ME"? IT MUST BE FROM CLIVE.

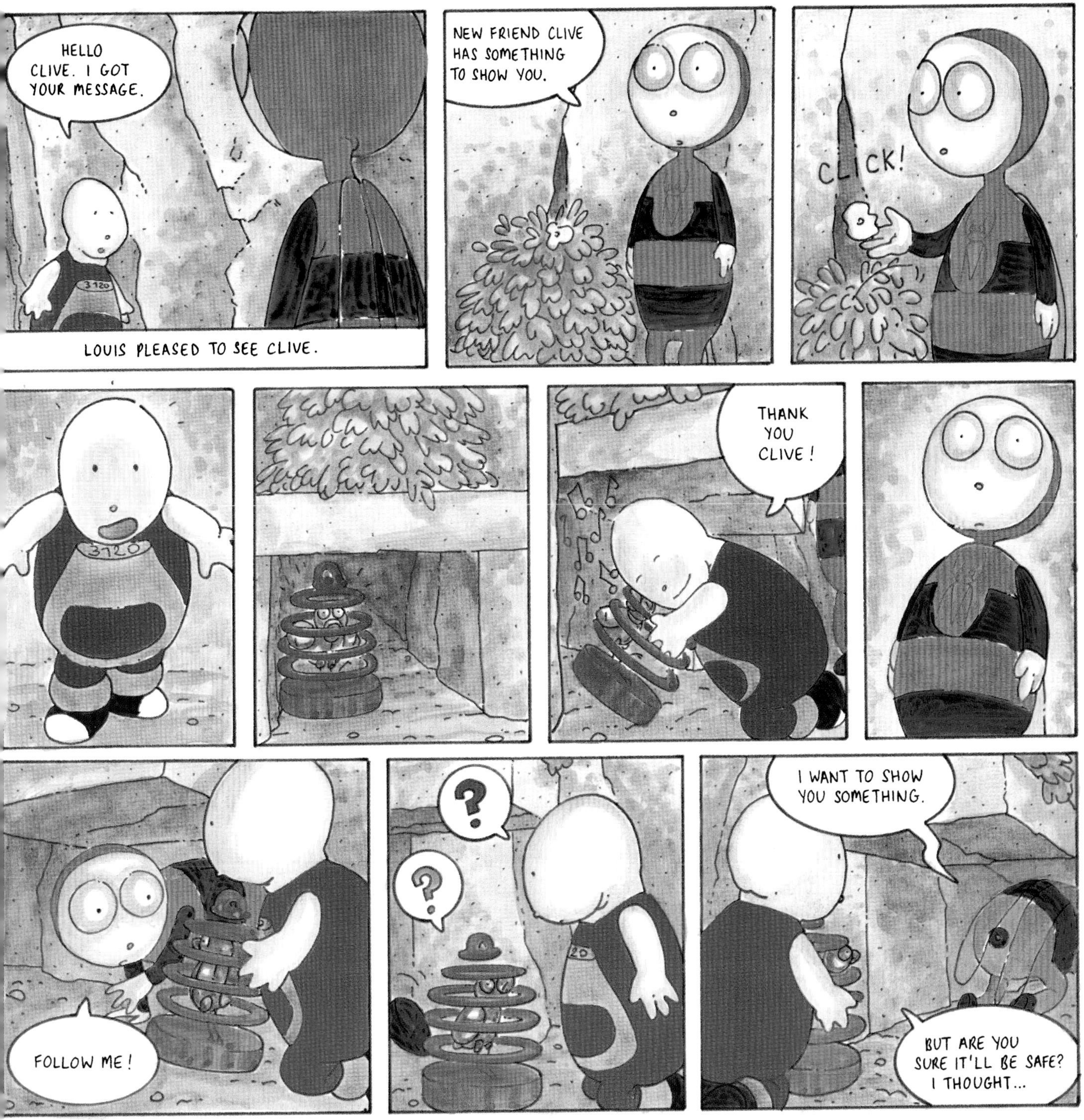
HELLO CLIVE. I GOT YOUR MESSAGE.
LOUIS PLEASED TO SEE CLIVE.
NEW FRIEND CLIVE HAS SOMETHING TO SHOW YOU.
CLICK!
THANK YOU CLIVE!
FOLLOW ME!
?
?
I WANT TO SHOW YOU SOMETHING.
BUT ARE YOU SURE IT'LL BE SAFE? I THOUGHT...

TRUST ME! I'M YOUR GOOD FRIEND.

NEW FRIEND CLIVE.

NEW FRIEND CLIVE.

CLIVE WAS BEHAVING STRANGELY. AS USUAL, LOUIS THOUGHT.

LET'S SEE WHAT CLIVE WANTS TO SHOW US.

CLICK!

?

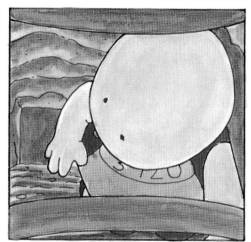

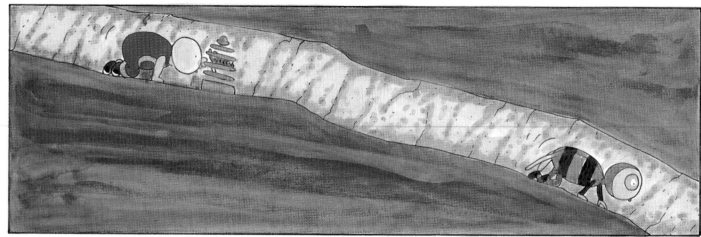

CRACKLE!

... STANDING NOW PROTECT THE QUEEN...

USE YOUR KNIFE TO SAVE HER LIFE.

CLIVE! ARE YOU ALL RIGHT?

CLIVE?

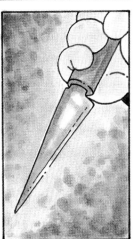

55

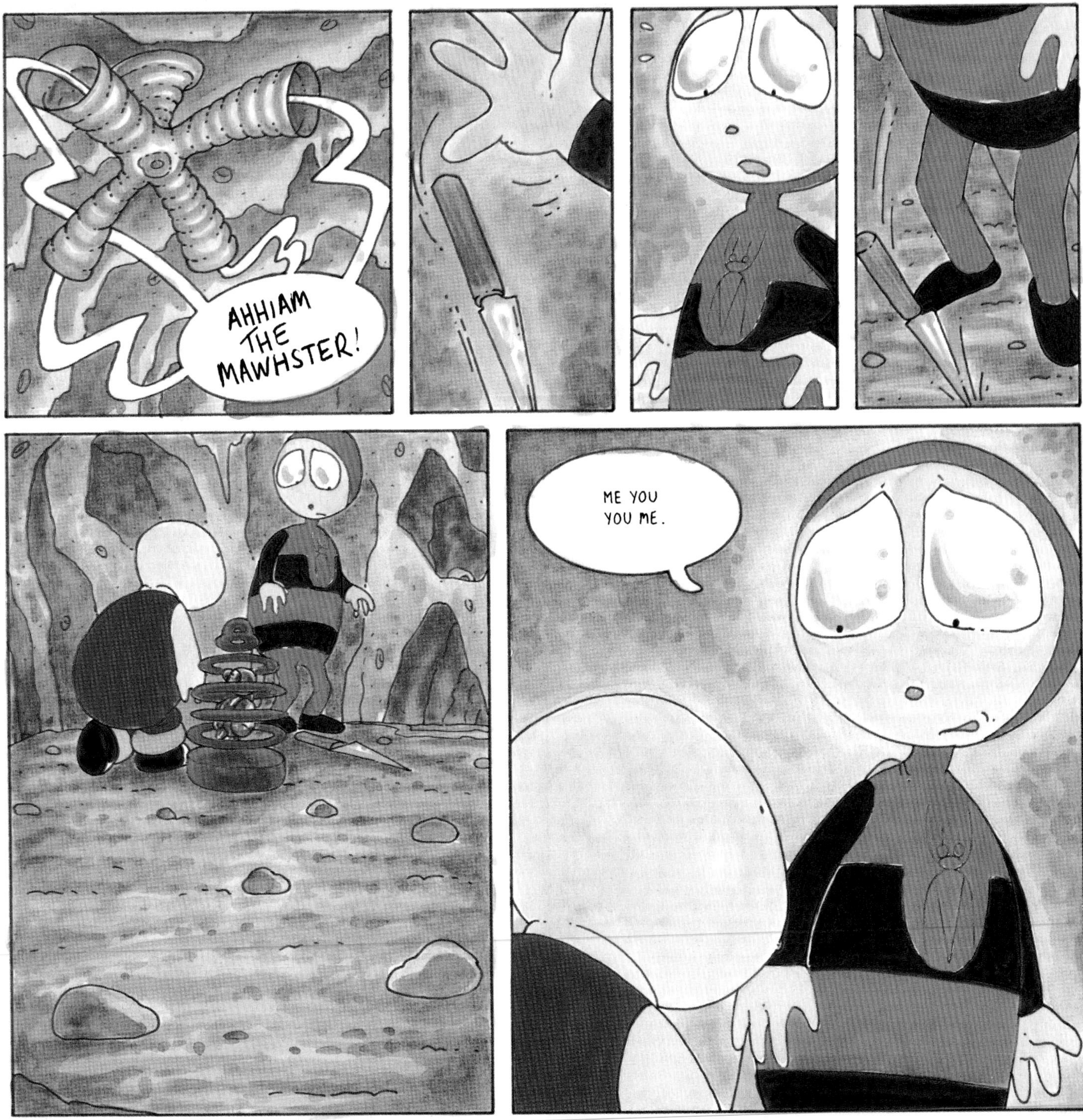
AHHIAM THE MAWHSTER!
ME YOU YOU ME.

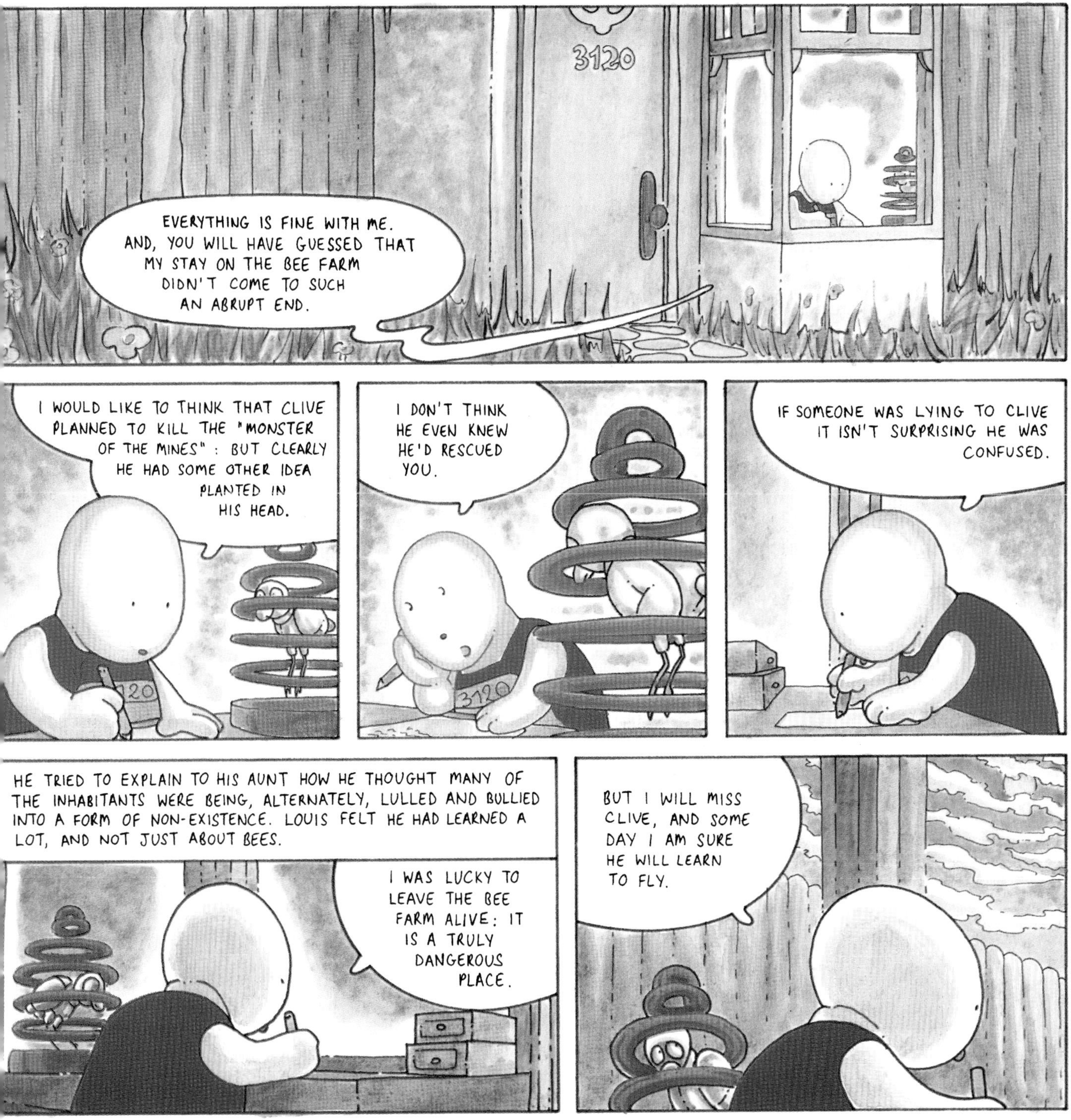
3120
EVERYTHING IS FINE WITH ME. AND, YOU WILL HAVE GUESSED THAT MY STAY ON THE BEE FARM DIDN'T COME TO SUCH AN ABRUPT END.
I WOULD LIKE TO THINK THAT CLIVE PLANNED TO KILL THE "MONSTER OF THE MINES" : BUT CLEARLY HE HAD SOME OTHER IDEA PLANTED IN HIS HEAD.
I DON'T THINK HE EVEN KNEW HE'D RESCUED YOU.
3120
IF SOMEONE WAS LYING TO CLIVE IT ISN'T SURPRISING HE WAS CONFUSED.
HE TRIED TO EXPLAIN TO HIS AUNT HOW HE THOUGHT MANY OF THE INHABITANTS WERE BEING, ALTERNATELY, LULLED AND BULLIED INTO A FORM OF NON-EXISTENCE. LOUIS FELT HE HAD LEARNED A LOT, AND NOT JUST ABOUT BEES.
I WAS LUCKY TO LEAVE THE BEE FARM ALIVE: IT IS A TRULY DANGEROUS PLACE.
BUT I WILL MISS CLIVE, AND SOME DAY I AM SURE HE WILL LEARN TO FLY.

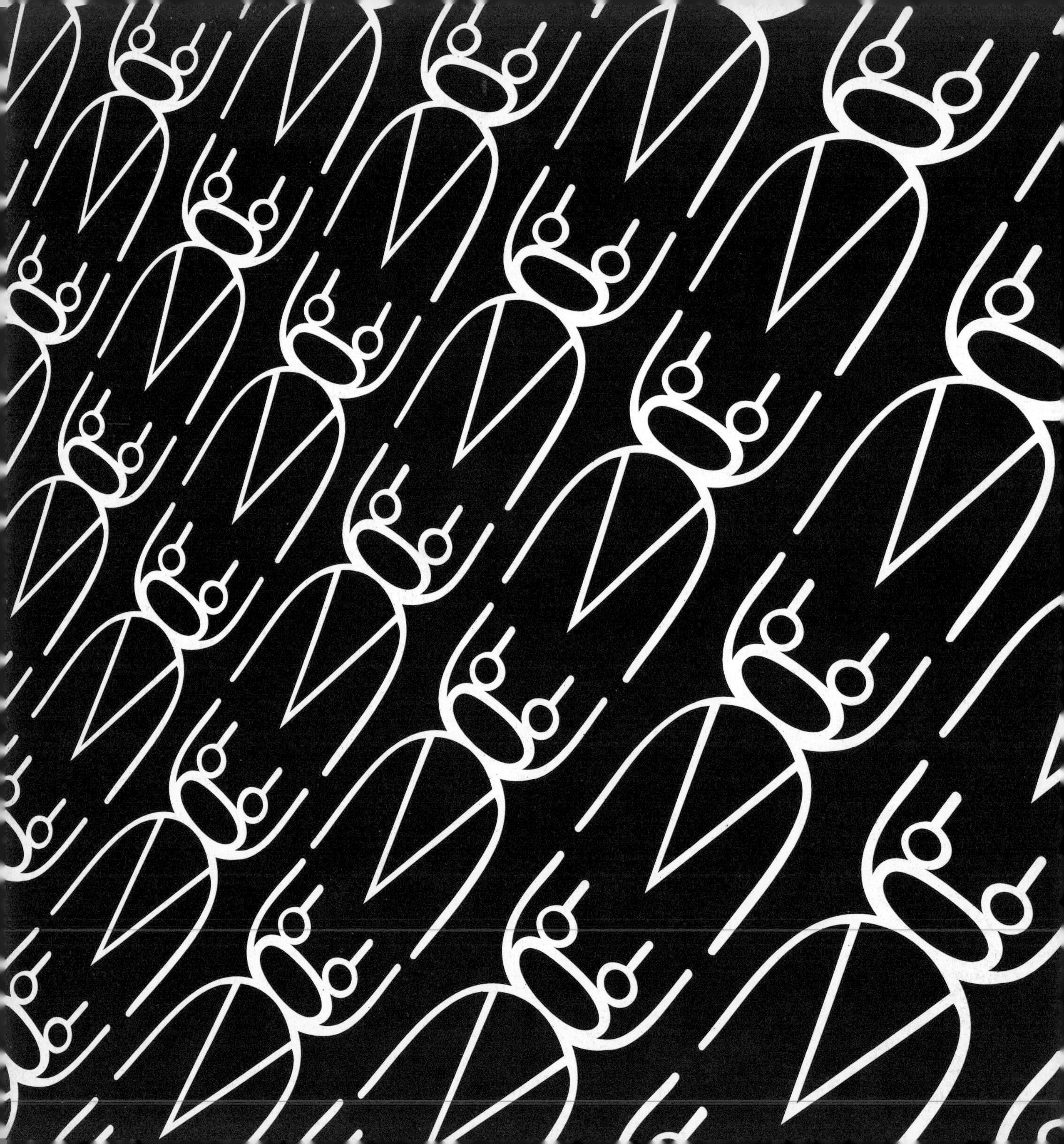